Lewis O Thompson

How to Conduct Prayer-Meetings

An account of some meetings that have been held

Lewis O Thompson

How to Conduct Prayer-Meetings
An account of some meetings that have been held

ISBN/EAN: 9783337144432

Printed in Europe, USA, Canada, Australia, Japan

Cover: Foto ©Lupo / pixelio.de

More available books at **www.hansebooks.com**

HOW TO CONDUCT PRAYER-MEETINGS,

OR

AN ACCOUNT OF SOME MEETINGS THAT HAVE BEEN HELD.

BY

REV. LEWIS O. THOMPSON,

AUTHOR OF THE "PRAYER-MEETING AND ITS IMPROVEMENT," ETC.

WITH AN INTRODUCTION BY

J. H. VINCENT, D. D.

BOSTON:
D. LOTHROP AND COMPANY,
FRANKLIN STREET, CORNER OF HAWLEY.

TO THE

REV. A. O. WRIGHT,

PRESIDENT OF THE "WISCONSIN FEMALE COLLEGE."

PREFACE.

The title of this book will distinguish it from "The Prayer-Meeting And Its Improvement," and designate it as a companion volume.

There are two agents which co-operate in religious worship — the human and the Divine. In the first volume I called attention to the fact that no meeting can be successful, from which the Divine agent is absent. "Without me ye can do nothing," "It is not by might nor by power, but by my Spirit, saith the Lord." In calling attention, then, in this volume, to such a variety of meetings that may be held for sustaining the interest and promoting a larger attendance, there is no intention of slighting Divine influences, nor of overlooking the need of humble reliance upon heaven for such guidance and inspiration in the meetings held, and the instrumentalities used, as alone can make them profitable.

Neither do I write as if I thought myself possessed of all the wisdom there is, on this subject. It has been my object to discover and describe such various meetings as my brethren in the ministry have found useful, hoping they may serve as helps in the Study of the Prayer-Meeting.

Of course it would be unfair to hold those who have so kindly favored me with their suggestions, responsible for any views of this book, other than those endorsed by their own handwriting. It would be a pleasure to know that their agreement is general, but whether there be agreement or difference, the obligations of the writer remain unchanged, and are hereby gratefully expressed.

If this book shall be in any sense, a help in the direction contemplated, I shall have many reasons for thankfulness.

May the Great Head of the Church, whose presence is promised to disciples gathered together in His name, accept this offering, pardon its imperfections, and bless for the promotion of spirituality and righteousness, whatever of suggestive good its pages may contain.

CONTENTS.

INTRODUCTION 11

CHAPTER I.
A HISTORY OF THE PRAYER-MEETING 17

CHAPTER II.
THE INFLUENCE OF THE PRAYER-MEETING . . . 40

CHAPTER III.
THE THEORY OF THE PRAYER-MEETING 49

CHAPTER IV.
THE REVIVAL PRAYER-MEETING. 51

CHAPTER V.
THE INQUIRY-MEETING HAS TAKEN ITS PLACE . 59

CHAPTER VI.
MOODY'S SCRIPTURE COUNSELS FOR INQUIRERS . . 67

CHAPTER VII.
THE VALUE OF TOPICS 84

CHAPTER VIII.
OBJECTIONS TO THEIR USE 88

CHAPTER IX.
OBJECTIONS CONSIDERED 93

CHAPTER X.
SOME OPINIONS OF PASTORS 99

CHAPTER XI.
SOME VIEWS OF MINISTERS 111

CHAPTER XII.
TYPICAL PRAYER-MEETINGS 123

CHAPTER XIII.
THE PRAYER-MEETING A GROWTH 134

CHAPTER XIV.
HOW SHALL WE GET MEMBERS TO TAKE PART? . . 138

CHAPTER XV.
MONTHLY CONCERT FOR MISSIONS 145

CHAPTER XVI.
A TEXT-MEETING 158

CHAPTER XVII.
A PROMISE-MEETING 167

CHAPTER XVIII.
AN EXPERIENCE-MEETING 172

CHAPTER XIX.
A CONSECRATION-MEETING 186

CHAPTER XX.
A THANKSGIVING PRAYER-MEETING 192

CHAPTER XXI.
MOODY'S PRAISE PRAYER-MEETING 198

CHAPTER XXII.
SONG SERVICE FOR THE PRAYER-MEETING . . . 213

CHAPTER XXIII.
METHODS FOR CONDUCTING BIBLE READINGS . . . 226

CHAPTER XXIV.
A Watch Prayer-Meeting 229
CHAPTER XXV.
Ladies' Prayer-Meetings 241
CHAPTER XXVI.
Tuesday Evening Meetings 248
CHAPTER XXVII.
Saturday Night Prayer-Meetings . . . 255
CHAPTER XXVIII.
Sunday Morning Meetings for Prayer . . 260
CHAPTER XXIX.
Childrens' Inquiry and Prayer-Meeting . . . 266
CHAPTER XXX.
Cottage Prayer-Meetings 273
CHAPTER XXXI.
The Family Meeting for Worship . . 280
CHAPTER XXXII.
Fulton Street Noonday Prayer-Meeting . . . 288
CHAPTER XXXIII.
The Chicago Noonday Prayer-Meeting . . . 297
CHAPTER XXXIV.
Prayer-Meeting Conventions 304
CHAPTER XXXV.
"Directory for Worship of the United Presbyterian Church" 309
CHAPTER XXXVI.
Moody's Seventeen Rules 311
CHAPTER XXXVII.
Different Forms of Printed Lists 314

INTRODUCTION.

There are three departments of the true church school: the *biblical* in the Sabbath-school; the *experimental* in the class or fellowship meeting; and the *devotional* in the prayer-meeting. In the first we look to God in His Word; in the second we look to God as He works within us; in the third we look to God himself, immediately, reverently, gratefully and supplicatingly.

The several elements of spiritual culture may be more or less blended in one service, as when in the prayer-meeting, personal experience is narrated and specific biblical themes studied; or, as in the Sabbath-school class, when a devout teacher in the study of the Word applies it to individual experience, under the guidance of the Holy Spirit, and leads his pupils to reverent worship under the impulse of the truth thus investigated and applied.

While usually, the threefold service may be more effectively rendered by distinct meetings, it is highly important that they should unite to a greater or less degree in every convocation of believers, whether for study, the relation of experience, or worship.

Every Christian should be interested in whatever tends to the increase of personal experience in the things of God, on the foundation of an intelligent apprehension of God's Word, and with the purpose of complete surrender to God; and there is no service more imperative to-day in connection with church activities, than that which shall increase the efficiency of these several branches of the school of the church.

A meeting of thoughtful men and women should have some thought given to it in advance, by him who is responsible for its conduct. Its object being sacred and important, its exercises must not be allowed to drift into superficial and stereotyped expressions.

If all good people were wise, and all thoughtful people had tact, we might be less careful about lines of thought by which devotional impulses and efforts are to be directed. There are devout, loyal, and faithful people, who are not endowed with the strongest kind of common sense. What they would be without the piety which holds them steady, we cannot say. That they are not perfect in judgment, does not militate against the Gospel which brings to them light, purpose and comfort. Their lack makes the leader's wisdom all the more important.

A wise minister will exercise judgment concerning the place of the prayer-meeting in the list of his church services. He will give it thought in advance — devout thought. He will come to it with strength of purpose, in the best possible physical and mental conditions. He will fully understand the perils and the dissipating power of apathy and worldliness, and seeking the right physical atmosphere in the place of meeting, he will also seek by personal influence, by wise direction, by sound sense, by believing prayer, to put a measure of human strength into the service, not as a substitute for, but as a medium, of the divine strength, without which the service itself would be a disastrous failure.

The author of this volume has given much thought to the questions involved in the regulation of the weekly meetings for prayer in the church. He has observed closely, experimented judiciously, consulted with persons of experience, pastors and others, and in this form brings to the church the results of his efforts.

The prayer-meeting can never be made a *popular* service, by which we mean a service attractive to unspiritual minds. It can never have the attractiveness of a concert or public church service, where music and sermon cater more or less to the tastes of the average worldling who frequents the sanctuary. Indeed, such popularity would be unfortunate. The prayer-meeting is a meeting of believers. This pre-supposes faith, spiritual tastes, fervent desire, and the habit of thoughtfulness in the lines of evangelical truth.

The prayer-meeting should not be dependent for its success upon good voices to read, pray or sing. The introduction of elocutionary and musical effects would do violence to the spirit of the occasion, and any attempt to turn the week evening prayer-meeting into a popular assembly will be injurious to the church.

The prayer-meeting will be profitable as its exercises are controlled by a leading thought, and the spontaneity of its services unrestrained. It must be both controlled and free. The control must be by indirection, and never too manifest. It is not a meeting of children, but of those who are sufficiently mature in thought and experience to know what they are about, and any obtrusive interference with personal freedom will work harm to all concerned.

The book, thus introduced to our attention, will commend itself to all Christian workers, by the practical sense, large experience, the careful observation and the deep religious purpose, which its author has brought to his aid in its preparation.

J. H. VINCENT.

Plainfield, N. J., Jan. 24, 1880.

HOW TO CONDUCT
PRAYER-MEETINGS.

CHAPTER I.

A History of the Prayer-Meeting.

THERE is a lack of literature on this subject. Either the sphere filled by this mid-week service has revolved so quietly about the church as to have passed almost unobserved, or the work done by it has accomplished so little for reviving and righteousness that there has scarcely been anything to observe. In many a church, the prayer-meeting is looked upon as a fifth wheel to its machinery. Careful investigation, however, will show us that the prayer-meeting is not a modern institution, and that there have been times when its sphere has been lighted up with unwonted brilliancy.

The most recent phase of the prayer-meeting to be noted, is the shape which it has taken within a few years past of publishing its topics with Scripture references, to be used either by a single church, or a number of churches in concert. Those churches that have engaged in the use of uniform subjects, find in this practice nothing to induce formality; nothing to dampen enthusiasm; nothing to beget hypocrisy and set phrases in speech; nothing to hinder the presence of the Holy Spirit that giveth life, and teacheth to pray; in a word, find in it nothing that "kills" a prayer-meeting, or says to its members stay at home. Far otherwise. It is this very thing of coming together in the prayer-meeting with the heart full of Scripture to illustrate the given subject, and of previous prayer upon it on the part of the membership that makes a meeting abound in zeal, in spirituality, and in heavenly refreshment. "Again, I say unto you, That if two of you shall agree on earth as touching anything that they shall ask, it shall be done for them of my Father which is in heaven." "If two of you shall agree"—and we cannot have a prayer-*meeting* with a smaller number than that—what stronger Scripture for a topical prayer-meeting do we require? The subject must be proposed and known before hand, before there can be agreement upon it, and does the promise become of no effect when the parties to it are not two merely, but a hundred, a thousand, or even a million? If agreement between two has its promise and advantage, surely agreement between a million praying Christians must also have its promise and its advantage multiplied to correspond with such numerical increase.

A uniform topical prayer-meeting is well defined in this text of Scripture — agreement with reference to what we shall ask of our Father in heaven — and let us not be afraid of such agreement, but rejoice the rather if it should meet with such fervor and adoption as ultimately to include all prayer-meeting churches.

All who are old enough, must have noticed how much nearer the evangelical churches of our land have been getting to each other, during the last three or four decades. What fierce controversies used to rage, and what bitter polemic sermons used to be hurled from pulpits against other denominations than our own!

I have just been told by a Christian gentleman in middle life, who belonged to the Old School before the re-union, that when he was a boy in Pennsylvania he was taught to believe "That a New School man was a bad man." Now what has wrought the wondrous change? I do not hesitate to answer — the Young Men's Christian Associations, uniform Sunday-school lessons, the Evangelical Alliance and the annual Week of Prayer; and, for my part, I do not doubt that uniformity in the texts of Scripture for the prayer-meetings, would intensify the fraternal spirit and bring all those who truly love the Lord Jesus Christ still nearer to each other.

Of the same nature with the topical meetings for prayer, as just intimated, are those meetings of concerted prayer for missions and the world's conversion, which are held annually, and had their origin in the second week of January, 1860. This meeting is of the same nature with the Monthly Concert for missions, which was established mainly through the influence and labors of Andrew Fuller in the last century, and with the Day of Prayer for missions which was held on the first Monday of January, for many years after 1830. The Monthly Concert is still very generally observed, and the Day of Prayer has been prolonged into the Week of Prayer, which is observed annually during the first week of January.

The Week of Prayer is the outgrowth of an intense piety contemplating the Saviour's command, the wretched condition of the heathen world, and the unrivalled facilities for travel, commerce, and international pursuits which modern inventions have opened.

The fact, that two-thirds of the world remain unchristian, is an obstacle in the path of the steamship, a bar across the track of the railway, a hindrance to the electric wire delighting to speak in all the tongues of men, and a delay to the stately tread of civilization. When grace and truth shall go abroad over the earth, then shall darkness and superstition flee away.

But why may not the world be evangelized? It is so commanded. Why may not the work be hastened? It is so promised to those that prosecute it prayerfully. Why, then, should not the Christians of to-day — the heroic one — third — seriously undertake the work as thus to be helped by steam, electricity, and the press, and as seriously pray for its successful issue? Let us of the nineteenth century undertake all this. We will do it, and as results we have already numerous missionary societies, Bible societies, and a week of concerted prayer. Would you know what utility the Week of Prayer subserves, go seek it in the lives of missionaries, in converted accessions to mission fields, and in the recorded requests and answers to prayer, with which our various missionary publications abound.

There is another feature of the modern prayer-meeting that ought not to be omitted, although its occurrence has been such a rarity that it lives in the remembrance of only a few, and that is the holding of prayer-meeting conventions. In 1858, a convention of this sort was held in Xenia, Ohio, to which invitations were very generally extended, and which was well attended during the few days that it was held. As only a very few meetings of this kind have been held, the reader may ask, "Why should we not hold prayer-meeting conventions, just as presbyteries, synods, general assemblies, conferences, associations, Bible institutes and Sunday-school parliaments are held, with stated regularity, to acknowledged utility and unquestioned increase of zeal and spirituality?" Why not? It is a fair question. The answer is doubtless found in the fact that a convention of this nature to amount to anything, requires a very high degree of praying piety, a very strong spirit of faith, an assured conviction that God answers prayer, and an indifference to the gibes and sneers that might be encountered in holding it, in the midst of a worldly-minded community. These things combine to make the undertaking as rare as it is arduous.

A few words in this place will suffice for those meetings now so successful, so well-known, and so numerously held in all the chief cities of Christendom, the business men's noonday prayer-meetings. The first one of this kind was the Fulton street noonday meeting, which was projected and fostered by the Consistory of the North Dutch Church, and their city missionary, Mr. J. C. Lanphier. It was begun as a weekly noonday meeting, and was held for the first time in a third-story room of the Old North Dutch Church in New York city, on Wednesday, September 23d, 1857.

"At twelve o'clock of that day," says the Rev. T. W. Chambers, "the door was thrown open and the missionary took his seat to await the response to the invitation that had been given. After a half-hour's delay, the steps of one person were heard as he mounted the staircase. Presently another appeared, and another, until the whole company amounted to six. On the next Wednesday, September 30th, the six increased to twenty, and the subsequent week, October 7th, as many as forty were present. During the interval between the first meeting and the third, Mr. Lanphier had consulted with Mr. Wilkin, the leading member of the Consistory, on the propriety of making the meeting semi-weekly or daily. It seemed to them that there was no good reason why, considering all the circumstances, enough persons should not be found in that part of the city who would be willing to come together for united prayer and praise every day. They accordingly determined to introduce this change, but were anticipated on the day of the third weekly meeting, by a similar proposition made and carried in the meeting itself."

The important change was made at once, the place

was transferred from the third story to the room below on the second, and on the eighth of October, 1857, was begun that great instrumentality of modern times, the noonday prayer-meeting, whose lines have already encircled the globe, whose interest has never abated, whose regularity neither war nor peace, neither rain nor snow has extinguished, and whose influence eternity alone can measure.

But we are now come to examine the origin of those prayer-meetings which the evangelical and reformed churches have been in the habit of holding on some evening in the mid-week, and it is safe to say that these have been held ever since those churches themselves were first established. The Methodist Church has been pre-eminently a prayer-meeting church.

"The awakenings," writes Dr. Thos. Huston, "which took place in various parts of England, under the ministry of Wesley and Whitefield, led to the establishment of social prayer-meetings; and, at this period, when within the pale of the National Establishment, and without it, all was under the torpor of spiritual death. This organization was a powerful means of exciting earnest minds to pursue after eternal concerns, and to impress them upon the serious attention of others."

We find, also, that the social prayer-meeting has been a time-honored and highly-prized instrumentality in the various branches of the Presbyterian Church throughout the world.

"When the prelatic persecution," observes Dr. Huston, "under Charles II., drove three hundred faithful Presbyterian ministers from their pulpits, and hireling curates were intruded upon their reluctant flocks, the value of private social prayer-meetings was again experienced, in upholding and comforting the servants of God, in evil times. Thus were they fitted for patient endurance of privations and suffering, and thus they were nerved for the noble conflict in which they engaged against Erastian power. In the latter part of the twenty-eight years' persecution, when under the cruel and arbitrary measures of the popish and bigoted James, the number of faithful witnesses was greatly reduced; and by indulgences and every other means that anti-christian policy could invent, apostacy and defection were encouraged, the few resolute covenanters who remained had resource to united prayer, and cultivated fraternal fellowship, as a precious means of preservation and safety amidst manifold danger and suffering. Hence, they were called 'The Society People;' and, the history of this disastrous period, whether as written by persons friendly or unfriendly to their cause, bears unequivocal testimony that it was, in a great measure, to their cordial intimate union, and to their faithful exertions, that the precious truths of the Gospel were preserved, and that the civil and religious liberties of Britain were rescued from the grasp of despotic rulers."

But the value of this meeting "of the people, for the people, and by the people," in maintaining vital godliness, had been discovered even earlier than this:

"This noble old church," writes Rev. J. B. Johnston, "the Church of Scotland — the mother of us all — not at all particularly singular here, but like most of the daughters of the Protestant Reformation, was born and nursed in the prayer-meeting. Protestantism, itself, is a social religion — a religion for the people; it flings away the shackles of papal tyranny from the conscience, puts the Bible into the hands of all, and opens for the masses free social intercourse and unrestricted Christian fellowship; and it points to the social prayer-meeting for its fullest enjoyment. The Church of Scotland, seems, from the very incipiency of her organization, to have recognized the claims of the prayer-meeting as a divine ordinance, more distinctly and formally than other churches of the Reformation, which retained more of the shadows of the

Romish ritualism. It is well-known to all familiar with its history, that the Church of Scotland received much of its distinctive character and spirit from its leading reformer, John Knox.

"While the reformer was a refugee from persecution in his own native land, he wrote from the continent in the year 1557, to his countrymen friendly to the cause of the Reformation, with the express view of calling the people to a leading and active part in the work, without and independently of the ruling powers both in the church and in the state. 'In October, following,' records Calderwood, 'he sent some letters to the Lords, and to particular gentlemen, wherein he proved that the reformation of religion and public enormities did appertain to more than to the clergy and chief rulers. His letters being read, it was concluded, after consultation, that they would prosecute their purpose once intended. That every one might be the more assured of the other, a common band was formed, wherein they promised before God, with their whole power, and hazard of their lives, to set forward and establish the true religion.' 'In this letter,' according to Dr. McCrie, 'he warmly recommended to every one the careful and frequent reading of the Scriptures. He inculcated the duty of attending to religious instruction and worship in each family.

He exhorted the brethren to meet together once every week, if practicable, and gave them directions for conducting their assemblies in the manner best adapted to their mutual improvement, while destitute of public teachers. They ought to begin with confession of sins, and invocation of the divine blessing. A portion of the Scriptures should then be read ; and they would find it of great advantage to observe a regular course in their reading, and to join a chapter of the Old and New Testament together. After the reading of the Scriptures, if an exhortation, interpretation, or doubt, occur to any brother, he might speak ; but he ought to do it with modesty, and a desire to edify, or to be edified, carefully avoiding multiplication of words, perplexed interpretation, and willfulness in reasoning. If, in the course of reading or conference, they met with any difficulties which they could not solve, he advised them to commit these to writing before they separated, that they might submit them to the judgment of the learned ; and he signified his own readiness to give them his advice by letters whenever it should be required. Their assemblies ought always to be closed, as well as opened, with prayer.'

"There is every reason to conclude that these directions were punctually complied with, and this letter, therefore may be viewed as an important document regarding the state of the Protestant Church in Scotland, previous to the establishment of the Reformation.' This letter certainly furnishes a remarkable directory for the government, order and exercises of the prayer-meeting among the laity."

And now the churches whose records have been thus examined, fail only in that they do not carry us far enough back. Is then, the people's meeting for prayer, praise and conference, no older than the sixteenth century? Let us see. If we cross over into Italy we shall find an interesting church existing there to-day, that is Protestant in its faith, and Presbyterian in its form of government — the Waldensian Church.

Now, "The Waldenses," writes Plumley, "dwelling in the valleys of Piedmont, in the extreme northwestern part of Italy, claim that from Christ and the apostles their fathers received the doctrines of God's word, as they have always believed them and the Presbyterian form of church government, as they have always in its simplicity maintained it.

"One of their earliest chroniclers, using the records and traditions of his people, asserts that 'the Waldenses are descended from those refugees who, after St. Paul had preached to them the Gospel, abandoned their beautiful country and fled — like the woman mentioned in the Apocalypse — to those wild mountains, where they have to this day handed down the Gospel from father to son, in the same purity and simplicity as it was preached to them.'

"In 1530, some pastors of the Waldenses wrote to the Reformers, who were just coming out of the Romish Church, to accept a purer faith, such as they had always believed, to this effect:

"'That you may at once understand the matter, we are a sort of teachers of a certain necessitous and small people, who, already, for more than four hundred years — nay, as those of our country frequently relate, from the times of the apostles — have sojourned among the most cruel thorns, yet as all the pious have easily judged, not without great favor of Christ.'"

History does not deny the claim that this people have ever been faithful to their motto — *lux in tenebris* — light in the darkness — and among them do we find that continuity in faith and practice which links the prayer-meeting of to-day as an organized instrumentality in the church, for the promotion of godliness with the times of the apostolic church. The historian of this people claim "that in all their emergencies, they had recourse to meeting for united prayer, as the great means of support and relief under long continued and severe persecution, and as the divinely appointed way of animating the hope of future de liverance. Ecclesiastical history records the marked attention of these early witnesses to this ordinance at different periods of their eventful history; and there can be no doubt that to it, in a large measure, are to be ascribed their remarkable unity in faith, and in godly practice, and their heroic constancy in sufferings. In the latter period of the Waldensian trials, shortly before the dawn of the Reformation, when 'darkness that might be felt,' had settled down upon the nations of Europe; when faithful witnesses had been almost wholly exterminated; when the voice of public protest against Rome's idolatry and oppression was nowhere distinctly heard throughout western Christendom, we have on record an affecting testimony to the value which the remnant of these ancient confessors still set upon the social prayer-meeting."

If this were all the evidence available, we might consider the connection complete with the apostolic church, but there are other sources, also. As the Roman Empire began to persecute those Christians that retained the primitive faith in its purity, they sought shelter in the catacombs of Rome and kept alive the sacred flame "in feeding on the word, and in united prayer and praise."

And, besides this, we are warranted in asserting, on the testimony of Pliny, that various bodies of Christians throughout the Roman Empire were in the habit of meeting for prayer and praise. In the year 103, when writing to the Emperor Trojan on the subject of persecution, he "earnestly dissuaded him from continuance in the enforcement of the edicts, and on the ground that the Christians were a harmless people, chargeable with no offence, only they were in the habit of meeting together to sing songs, and to worship Christ as God."

Thus the chief support of religion during those years of persecutions when the Cæsars wielded the Roman Empire as an engine for the destruction of Christianity, was derived from those meetings for song and prayer which they held — those meetings held in secret, at night or early morn, where were gathered together the faithful band to pray and sing to Christ as their Saviour. It was by meetings such as these that they formed and kept alive the sacred flame of piety — that flame which was afterward to light up the gloom of the catacombs with the hope of heaven and immortality; it was by the instrumentality of their prayer-meetings that this holy flame was nourished which was to shine so brightly among the Waldenses and relieve the gloom of the dark ages, and which by the grace of God has been so replenished that it now freely burns and shines from all the hilltops, and in all the valleys of Christendom. As a result, the church of to-day has become a great power, her light shining clear as the sun, beautiful as the moon, and terrible as an army with banners. Surely, had the Cæsars known it, that which to Pliny seemed most harmless and insignificant — the assembling of the disciples to continue steadfastly in prayer — was the very thing they ought to have feared most of all — for in these prayer-meetings was forged that power which shattered the Roman eagle, and destroyed the old-time Paganism.

But even if all these sources should fail us, as usually relied upon, and we could trace the prayer-meeting back no farther than the sixteenth century, can we leap over the gap and find any meeting to correspond with it in the apostolic church? Is the prayer-meeting a modern institution like the Sabbath-school, which is just now completing its first centennial; or, is it founded and established in the word and ordinances of God?

In Acts, Chapters one and two, we find the record of the first and longest prayer-meeting in the history of the Christian church. The eleven disciples were assembled in an upper room in Jerusalem, and "continued with one accord in prayer and supplication, with the women, and Mary, the mother of Jesus, and with his brethren" to "wait for the promise of the Father," and having thus waited through ten days, when "Pentecost was fully come," the promised blessing was given unto them, and the descending flame of God anointed their lips and hearts, and fully endued them with power for their life-work of preaching Christ, and him crucified, risen and ascended into heaven. Nor was this their only prayer-meeting. A short time afterward, being again assembled, "when they had prayed, the place was shaken where they were assembled together; and they were all filled with the Holy Ghost, and they spake the word of God with boldness." (Acts 4 : 31.)

Again, when Peter was imprisoned the brethren came together "in the house of Mary, the mother of John," to pray for help and deliverance — a topical prayer-meeting — and, lo! whilst they were continuing their supplications, the answer to their prayers stood without in living form, knocking at the door of the house for admittance that he might declare unto "them how the Lord had brought him out of the prison." (Acts 12 : 5–17.)

The Book of Acts clearly teaches that meetings for prayer were frequently and regularly held from house to house, to the evident increase of their numbers, or in more secluded places, or by the side of some water-course. (Acts 16 : 13.)

But we are even to believe that the Saviour was in the habit of holding meetings for prayer and instruction with the disciples. We read in the Gospel that Christ was a man of prayer. He taught his disciples to pray, even as John Baptist had also taught his. Olivet and Gethesmane were places frequently chosen for these meetings of prayer. "Prayer with his disciples apart, secluded from the multitudes, was by him and others formed into a religious habit. It was in this school of prayer and religious conference — for their prayer-meetings were conference meetings — that the disciples were trained for that active and religious work of revival in which they were afterwards employed, and which turned the world upside down."

If we read the Epistles, we shall discover that these meetings for prayer were continued by the churches which the apostles had established. "The church in the house," is twice mentioned, and refers naturally and beautifully to the prayer-meetings that were held in the house of some faithful brother or sister. We may well believe that the church at Rome, Corinth, Colosse, or elsewhere, was distinguished for its fidelity to the apostle's word and example, continuing steadfast in prayers, and the breaking of bread from house to house, and not altogether following the example of some who forsook the assemblies for prayer.

In Chapters twelve, thirteen and fourteen of First Corinthians, Paul gives some directions for the proper employment by the church of the various spiritual gifts of its members. "How is it then, brethren?" asks the apostle, "when ye come together, every one of you hath a psalm, hath a doctrine, hath a tongue, hath a revelation, hath an interpretation, Let all things be done unto edifying."

They are to be orderly in the parts and exercises of the prayer-meeting, that all might be done to the edifying of the brethren, and to the good of such strangers as might be present. Now, prayer as to its nature, is always the same, but the occasions for offering it, may greatly vary. The following different occasions with more or less clearness, may be enforced by the teachings of Scripture:

1. Prayer in secret. (Matt. 6; 6.)

2. Prayer in the family. (Dan. 6: 10; Acts 10: 30; Ps. 55: 17.) Possibly the "church in the house," (Rom. 16: 5; I. Cor. 16: 19.) may mean the gathering together the household for prayer. An inference also, may be derived from the use of the word "ye," in Matt. 6: 7.

3. Prayer in the social gatherings of the elect, as

distinct from the services of the Christian as these had been based upon the model of the services in the synagogue. (Acts 1 : 14; Acts 4 : 31 ; Acts 12 : 5 Acts 16 ; 13 ; etc.)

4. Private prayer in synagogue or the temple. (Matt. 6 : 5 ; Luke 18 ; 10.)

5. Public prayer in the temple. (II. Chron. 6 : 14–42.)

And if it be asked what became of the early prayer-meeting when Christianity planted the banner of the cross upon the ruins of the Roman panthenon and the coliseum, we may answer in brief that as the church became great and powerful by its alliance with the empire, it was corrupted by the incorporation of unconverted men — of men christened, but not christianized — who united with it, caring nothing for piety and vital godliness, but a great deal for power and self-aggrandizement. It was then that those meetings from house to house, for conference, prayer and praise, became antiquated, and the Roman Church in its hierarchy entered upon that career of usurpation and spiritual tyranny that has well-nigh resulted in the total subversion of a free Gospel and a pure faith.

The same tendency is manifest in any local Protestant Church to-day, when its members become cold and indifferent. But little is thought of the prayer-meeting, only a few attend, the fires upon the social altar burn low, and both they and the world think, "of what use or avail is such a meeting as this?"

It was for some such reason that the prayer-meeting was never incorporated into the Romish Church, or that having been incorporated, it was destroyed by the worldly spirit of a usurping priesthood, and the indifference of a worldly-minded membership. There is to-day in this Church too great a distance between the priests and the people, between bishops, cardinals and pope, to admit of such equality and fraternity as the social meeting for conference, prayer and praise would introduce. It is true the Roman Catholic Church is always open for prayer, but is not for the fellowship prayer-meeting in which the people shall be permitted to pray to Christ as their Saviour, in such words as the Spirit shall then and there teach them to utter. It is open, the rather, for private prayer, (and that so far as it goes is well enough) for the counting of beads, the adoration of saints, the sprinkling of holy water, the confessional and priestly absolution (and these so far as they go have little spiritual value, because they usurp the place of Christ). Let but the Romish Church give to its people an open Bible, and open their churches and cathedrals for social prayer and praise, and who does not see that primitive piety would be revived, or as great a revival of religion in that church would take place, as was witnessed when, under the lead of the reformers, the Bible was given to the people, and the apostolic prayer-meeting was re-established?

And thus, the prayer-meetings of Christ, of the apostles, and of the early Christian churches by them founded, holds out a historic link, to which may be fastened the meetings for song and prayer which Pliny mentioned, the meetings held in the catacombs of Rome, the meetings of the pious and heroic Waldenses, the restored meetings of the sixteenth century, and the meetings for social prayer which your church holds, and which you are in the habit of attending.

CHAPTER II.

The Influence of the Prayer-Meeting.

IT is evident, from the sketch I have just given, that the state of vital godliness in any church or denomination, at any time of its history, may be inferred from its prayer-meetings, and the place they have filled at the time considered. Seasons of spiritual prosperity have been times when social prayer predominated.

Its influence upon the church itself is as various as the manifestations of its life, faith, and hope. At the foundation of all healthful activity in the prayer-meeting will be found the habit of secret prayer. It is secret prayer that builds up a strong and robust individual Christian character. It is a significant fact that all the truly great men of the church — men whose lives have been to the earth as its saving salt, from righteous Abel down to the present — have been men of secret prayer, who like Enoch have walked with God during all their life. The first mark of Saul's conversion is stated by the evangelist to have been, "Behold, he prayeth." With the statement of that convincing proof,

Ananias ceased to be afraid of one who had hitherto, as the great enemy of the new faith, made havoc of the church.

"I fear," said Mary, Queen of the Scots, "the prayers of John Knox more than an army of ten thousand men."

The second great reformation of the modern church had its origin in that little band of praying students at Oxford, composed of Whitefield, the two Wesleys, and twelve others — a movement in its importance scarcely second to any in the whole history of the church. We need not seek far to find the sources of that mighty power which Whitefield wielded. "Whenever I knelt down," said he, "I felt great pressure both on soul and body; and have often prayed under the weight of them till the sweat came through me. God only knows how many nights I have lain upon my bed, groaning under what I felt. Whole days and weeks have I spent in lying prostrate on the ground, in silent or vocal prayer."

It is prayer that gives healthy arterial blood to the spiritual man, and makes him a power for righteousness that surpasses an army of prayerless Christians. It is by prayer that the man of God takes hold of unseen spiritual forces that originate at the throne of God, and move, shake, and control the world in the interests of grace and salvation, of faith and active godliness. Oh, for an army of praying fathers and mothers! Oh, for a cohort of praying Luthers, Whitefields, and Wesleys! Oh, for a band of men and women like Simeon and Anna, to spend days and nights in prayer; for such as these find what Archimedes vainly sought, a standing place from which to move the world, and then should we witness, even in our day, the birth-throes of Pentecost.

> "Prayer makes the darkened clouds withdraw,
> Prayer climbs the ladder Jacob saw,
> Gives exercise to faith and love,
> Brings every blessing from above.
>
> Restraining prayer we cease to fight;
> Prayer makes the Christian's armor bright;
> And Satan trembles when he sees
> The weakest saint upon his knees."

If this be so, what an influence for good is allowed to lie dormant in our churches in connection with their prayer-meetings. It is the opinion of Moody, that in nothing does the church of to-day more fail, than in the holding of her prayer-meetings. "I have noticed," he said in the New York Hippodrome, "that in travelling up and down the country, and after mingling with a great many ministers, that it is not the man that can preach the best that is the most successful, but the man that knows how to get his people together to pray. He has more freedom. It is so much easier to preach to an audience that is in full sympathy with you, than to those who are criticising all the time. It chills your heart through and through. Now, if we could only have our prayer-meetings what they ought to be, and get people to go, not out of any sense of duty, but because they delight to go, it would be a great help to a minister in his Sunday services."

The prayer-meeting, likewise, has its influence upon the social life of the church. Prayer, song and religious conference, are evidences of the highest spiritual fellowship and communion that saints enjoy here below. There is in these meetings the power of sympathy and oneness that make them a reflex image of that larger and nobler meeting above, where is fulness of joy and pleasures forever more.

The influence of the prayer-meeting is still farther seen in this, that it promotes the spirit of revival and beneficence. Modern missions had their birth in a a revived piety; "nor can it be denied," observes Rev. J. B. Johnston, "that revivals are the offspring of prayer. God's Spirit prepares for revival and for mission work — as for every other good work — first by pouring out upon His people a spirit of grace and supplication. This leads them to the prayer-meeting, to ask, in concert, for a revival; they are revived, and so fitted for every good work, in answer to prayer. That the missionary spirit of modern times, which has revolutionized the church, and which is now turning the world upside down, caught its inspiration from the revival of religion, no one conversant with the history of the times will doubt. It is equally true, that the revival of religion and of missions, both received their new impulses from the life-invigorating spirit of prayer — social and concerted prayer, eminently. Their historic connection and spiritual affinity are clearly traceable, awarding to the prayer-meeting that awakening power which has vigorously put into operation those world-renowned agencies (Tract, Bible and Missionary Societies), which are now so gloriously, under the Captain of our Salvation, evangelizing the world."

American missions were born in prayer and the prayer-meeting. "By means of this influence," says Dr. Humphrey, "Mills prevailed to diffuse, through a circle of choice spirits, that zeal for missions which actuated his own breast. On Wednesday afternoons they used to retire for prayer to the bottom of a valley, south of the west college and on Saturday afternoons, when they had more leisure, to the more remote meadow on the bank of the Hoosack, and there, under the hay-stack, those young Elijahs prayed into existence the embryo of American missions. They carried this with them to Andover, where it has roused into missionaries many that have gone to the heathen, and where it is still exerting a powerful influence on the interests of the world. I have been in situations to know, that from the counsels in that sacred conclave — the prayer-meeting in the valley and under the hay-stack — or from the mind of Mills himself, arose the American Board of Commissioners for Foreign Missions, and also the American Bible Society, and the United Foreign Missionary Society."

Its influence goes out to the community in which the prayer-meeting is held, and out beyond that to the mission stations of the world. We may take the history of the Fulton street noon day meeting as an example of its far-reaching power for good, and a type for the model prayer-meeting.

Dr. Prime, the esteemed editor of the *N. Y. Observer*, has written three books, "The Power of Prayer," "Five Years of Prayer," and "Fifteen Years of Prayer," in which he has graphically and eloquently depicted some of the more remarkable conversions connected with that meeting. "Five years ago" wrote Dr. Prime in 1863, in the introductory chapter to his second book on prayer, "'The Power of Prayer,' was published. It was hailed with wonderful interest in this country and abroad. It was republished in England and Scotland; widely circulated in Wales and Ireland; two translations were printed in France, and another in the East, and more than a hundred thousand copies distributed and read. In many places in this, and foreign countries, public meetings were held, and chapters read from it to quicken the desire and faith of Christians, and to encourage them in prayer for the outpouring of the Holy Spirit. In a large number of villages and rural congregations, revivals of religion followed the reading of these remarkable facts. The author has a letter now in his hands, addressed to him from a foreign land, informing him that its perusal had resulted in the conversion of *a pastor* and a precious revival in his church. Requests for prayer in behalf of individuals and communities have reached them in various languages, and from all parts of the world where the knowledge has gone of what God is doing for His people here, in answer to their petitions.

"That publication was made after the Fulton street prayer-meeting had been in existence one year. Within that brief season the record was so gracious and glorious as to fill heaven and earth with joy. Now that five years more have passed away, bearing with them the fruits of Christian labor and prayer, it has seemed to many, that duty to Him who hears and answers prayer, requires that another report should be made. A vast number of facts have accumulated which are well authenticated, and having been tested by time, the genuineness of the results is established."

If you would know what the influence of a truly spiritual prayer-meeting is, and ought to be, you have only to read the glowing pages of these three books, and full conviction will follow. There is, in the handful of earnest praying Christians, meeting week by week, an instrumentality of tremendous spiritual force which, if rightly directed, might be used for the awakening of an entire community. No more need be said in this connection, than that the seasons in which the church has spiritually prospered, are the seasons when the prayer-meeting has kindled anew the flames of devotion and revival. I need not here more than say that the prayer-meeting has its influence upon the pastorate; has its influence upon the organic life of the church; has its influence upon the active piety of its membership; has its influence upon family life and family religion; has its influence upon the spiritual work of the Sabbath-school. I need not here more than say, that under its heavenly spirit it originates multiplied forms of charity and self-denial for the good of others; that it originates and fosters a spirit of missions; that it establishes and perpetuates Tract and Bible Societies; that it forms and maintains various other organizations for evangelical labor, both at home and abroad.

What then, in view of all this, ought to be the place which such an institution as this ought to hold in your confidence and esteem; what ought to be the place which the prayer-meeting of your church and attendance ought to occupy in the midst of the community where it has been planted? Is there nothing that you can do by which to improve the spirituality of your prayer-meeting, and lift it still higher in its usefulness and reviving power? Shall it not receive from you, and does it not demand, your best thoughts, your prayers, your presence, and spirit-directed co-operation? And still —

> "What various hindrances we meet
> In coming to a mercy-seat!
> Yet who that knows the worth of prayer
> But wishes to be often there."

CHAPTER III.

THE THEORY OF THE PRAYER-MEETING.

IT will help us in the conduct of the prayer-meeting, if we get a correct theory of what kind of a meeting it ought to be. Is it a "revival service" for the conversion of the impenitent; or, in the main, a meeting of Christians for conference and edification? Whether it is one or the other will depend upon the class of persons who attend the regular prayer-meeting. The usual prayer-meeting, as a rule, is attended by professing Christians. It is rarely the case that non-professors of religion drop in; they do it, occasionally, as a matter of curiosity, or to oblige friends, and the like — not that they are not welcome; but I speak of what is the custom. And if the usual prayer-meetings of the church, year in and year out, are mainly the meetings of Christians, then the services in their nature ought to be shaped more with reference to the spiritual interests of those who come, than with reference to those who rarely, or never come.

If this view be correct, then the usual services ought to consist of a Scripture lesson, and opportunities for prayer, praise, exhortation, the narration of experience, the expression of testimony to the power of Christian truth and grace in times of trial, temptation, and victory, and such references from the Scripture lesson, with illustrations from facts, principles, and experience, as shall tend to develop the Christian gifts of the church, and build up a holy character in its members. The prayer-meeting is a training-school for the promotion of godliness, the increase of love, the strengthening of faith, the quickening of hope, and the stirring up the mind of the brethren to renewed zeal, diligence and fidelity in the work of the Lord.

Such questions, then, as who are the people that habitually attend, what is their number, what has been Christian nurture, who are those who take part in its exercises, and how many are there with speaking and praying gifts to be cultivated, will lead us to the true theory for our own prayer-meetings. Whether it shall be a "social prayer-meeting," or a "revival prayer-meeting," will depend very much upon what we, with God's help, shall make it; for we ought to hold no other theory than one whose workings will spiritually improve those who attend, and all who can be induced to attend.

CHAPTER IV.

THE REVIVAL PRAYER-MEETING.

A WRITER, who very kindly reviewed "The Prayer-Meeting and its Improvement," in *Scribner's Monthly*, for Feb., 1879, remarked that the ideal prayer-meeting of this book "is what one may call revivalistic." How far this remark is applicable, will depend upon the precise meaning given to the term "revivalistic." I think, however, quite a difference will be observed between the social prayer-meeting, and what has generally been known as the revival prayer-meeting, if a brief description of the nature and methods of the latter be here introduced.

In 1840, the Rev. Robert Young, a Wesleyan minister, published in London a tractate whose object was to remove prejudices against the revival prayer-meeting, and to offer some suggestions for its conduct. This prayer-meeting was always held after a preaching service.

"My general plan," he wrote, "is to close the regular

service, that those persons may withdraw who think proper to do so. I then commence the service of the prayer-meeting by singing a hymn; and when the persons withdrawing have left the chapel, I request a leader or local preacher to pray. After prayer I deliver a short address, and urge upon every sinner present, as God may give me ability, the necessity of an immediate attention to the concerns of the soul, and affectionately invite all who may be convinced of sin, and willing to make an entire surrender of themselves to God on Gospel terms, to come forward to the place assigned for penitents, with the view of obtaining mercy; explaining, at the same time, my reasons for the plan recommended. Generally there is a solemn pause for a short time; then one and another come forward with anxious looks, and some with bitter tears, to humble themselves before the Lord. A hymn suited to the occasion is next sung by the congregation, and in the meantime all that have presented themselves as seekers of salvation are spoken to, and instructed according to their respective conditions. Earnest prayer is now offered to God for them, and in the course of an hour or two, generally speaking, most of them profess to obtain redemption through the blood of Christ, even the forgiveness of their sins, and, like the publican go down to their houses justified. Never more than one person at the same time is permitted to pray aloud; nor is the practice of singing tunes at the same time ever tolerated. And if on any occasion there are indications of mere animal excitement, all present are requested to take their seats, excepting the penitents, who still remain kneeling, and I address them on subjects likely to lead to solemn and orderly devotion; and I have never known such a measure fail in producing the desired effect. My usual plan is likewise to deliver two or three short and pointed addresses during the meeting, in which the penitents are not only directed and encouraged, and the plan of salvation simplified, but the congregation cautioned against resisting the influence graciously vouchsafed, and invited and urged to cooperate with God in earnestly praying for the conversion of those whom He has convinced of sin."

And against the objection that a service of this kind following the sermon, threw the affairs of the household into disorder, and disarranged domestic duties, he stated, that such meetings ought never "on any occasion, to be held later than ten o'clock, and never so late as that, unless there be a very special influence felt. The heads of families engaging in them should invariably have family worship before they come to the evening service, that no loss at home may be sustained by their exertions in the prayer-meeting. This plan, I know, is adopted by many excellent prayer-leaders with good effect."

And to the question why such meetings as these were not more generally conducted by all pious ministers of the Gospel, he replied, that all might not be convinced of their utility. One who has never held such meetings has been pre-prejudiced against them by the representations he has heard from others; "or, perhaps, he has been present at such meetings, where no minister or competent person took their management, and has been shocked with their disorder and apparent irreverence; or he may possibly have known persons accustomed to take a prominent part in such assemblies, not so upright in their walk and conversation as they ought to have been, and has therefore felt disgusted. Another reason may be found in the pride of intellect. It is a very prevailing opinion, that for a minister to engage in a prayer-meeting after preaching, and endeavor to get the people saved before they leave the sanctuary, is a very unintellectual thing, and that none but ministers of a low grade of intellect will countenance it.

"I once heard a very highly esteemed individual say that he did not want a prayer-meeting revivalist for his minister, but an intellectual man. How far this opinion is founded in truth, I shall not now stop to inquire, it being enough for my present purpose merely to state that such an opinion most certainly exists; and, in all probability, it is the chief reason which prevents some men from engaging in revival prayer-meetings; for it must require much grace for a man of brilliant parts to be made willing to be counted a fool for Christ's sake; and not the less for those who desire to be considered as possessing those parts, to submit to a mode of working that is deemed so unintellectual. But there is another cause, not yet mentioned, which operates, I have no hesitation in saying, to prevent other ministers from engaging in revival prayer-meetings — they are convinced of their utility, would be willing to endure any reproach in the path of duty, and do anything to save souls; but they think they have no adaptation for this kind of work, and are thereby deterred from engaging in it. I know this is the case with some of my most esteemed brethren in the ministry, the latchet of whose shoes I am unworthy to unloose. Nor should it be forgotten that the conducting of such meetings, after a hard day's labor, such as Wesleyan ministers generally have on the Sabbath, required a physical energy which every man does not possess; and some who possess it, choose to meet the society according to Mr. Wesley's directions, to administer special advice, and thus endeavor to perform the very important work of building up and establishing the church, rather than engage in a service for which they feel themselves less qualified."

Mr. Young did not claim to be successful in all those meetings, but the cause of his failure and disappointment he found to exist "in the sins and imperfections of man. For several years, I have, on an average, held annually about forty such meetings; and in all those meetings, with the exception of four, some persons have professed to obtain salvation. In one of the meetings, where no apparent good was done, there was manifestly too much confidence placed in man, and God therefore withheld his blessing; and in another, the wildness of an untutored people, that could not be controlled, evidently grieved the Holy Spirit, and prevented good from being effected."

And his revival prayer-meetings of this kind were generally followed by a brief religious conversation, conducted by two or three pious and judicious class-leaders in an adjoining vestry, where the converts "might, in the absence of excitement, endeavor to ascertain how far the work was genuine. There was also a person in the vestry to take the addresses of such professed converts, with the view of their being visited in the course of the week at their own houses. A correct list of the persons thus obtained, was sent to the leaders' meeting on Wednesday evening, where it was divided among the leaders, who kindly engaged to visit all the persons whose names were found on that list, with the view of encouraging their hearts in the Lord, and of getting them to meet in class, if not already connected with some section of the Christian Church. Those who did not really seem to have found peace with God, in these conversations, received a little book called 'The Serious Inquirer After Salvation, Affectionately Addressed,' which simplified the way of salvation; and those whose case seemed more hopeful, received a little book called 'The New Convert, Directed and Encouraged.'

"The date of the year, and the name of each individual, receiving either of these books, were inscribed thereon, and if he should after prove unfaithful, the little book, with its inscription, might, by the blessing of God, recall to his mind impressions and enjoyments lost, and thus, as an humble monitor, lead him again to repentance."

I have also quoted thus at length from one who so highly valued this method, that each leader of a prayer-meeting may decide for himself how far such exercises could be profitably conducted by him and his people. This matter admits of trial by those who think that the services of the regular prayer-meeting should be strictly revivalistic. With many mid-week prayer-meetings, are connected a variety of peculiar circumstances, liable to arise as hindrances. As a general thing, not one-half, nor one-fourth, it may be, of the church membership, attend regularly the prayer-meeting. Then, again, there is but a very small number trained or qualified to take part in the exercises. And still farther, to this meeting the unconverted never, or but rarely come. In cases of this kind, it seems judicious to adapt the services to the spiritual needs of those who habitually come, than with reference to those who are habitually absent. But if a service of this kind can be kept up continuously the entire year, and then year after year by the same leader, in a country charge, or in a small community, or even in a city, and each meeting, or at least as a rule, resulting in the conversion of one or more persons, then surely he who on trial finds the revival prayer-meetings thus sustained and profitable, need not seek any other method for their conduct; for their utility is demonstrated in his case by an experience that must be conclusive.

CHAPTER V.

THE INQUIRY-MEETING HAS TAKEN ITS PLACE.

SO far as is known to me, the inquiry-meeting has now very generally taken the place of what was described in the preceding chapter as the revival prayer-meeting. It seems to me that each class of meetings — the inquiry-meeting and the regular prayer-meeting — is profitable, and has its own sphere, so that neither one should be omitted, nor both of them merged into the revival prayer-meeting. And, with the object in view of presenting the inquiry-meeting as an auxiliary to pastoral and prayer-meeting work, it may not be out of place to introduce here the experience of those who have found it an indispensable aid in this direction, and sketch in outline several methods by which inquiry-meetings have been successfully conducted. It is hardly necessary to add that the so-called evangelists of our day invariably follow all their preaching services with an inquiry-meeting, generally held in an adjoining room, and assisted by Christian workers who are skilled in the use of the Word of God.

The first method will show how even a pastor, who is regularly settled in his charge, may avail himself of a service of this kind. Rev. Henry C. Fish, of Newark, N. J., related his experience in this direction, at the "ministerial convention" held in New York city in 1876, in connection with the revival labors of Moody and Sankey.

"I do not know," said he, "why I have been selected by Mr. Moody to open this discussion, except it be from the fact that I have long been connected with inquiry-meetings, and that of the twelve hundred conversions that have taken place in connection with my ministry of the last twenty-five years, almost the whole of that number have come into the light of the Gospel through the agency of such meetings. I feel that a great part of my ministry has been wasted for lack of this very agency; and I have now resolved that no service shall pass, except under very extraordinary circumstances, which shall not be followed by an inquiry-meeting. Standing by the Sea of Galilee on one occasion, and seeing its waters teeming with fish, I remembered what Christ said to his disciples on that very lake: 'I will make you fishers of men;' and coming back to my church I told them the inquiry-meeting is the best place to 'catch souls;' and that ought to be the one object of our preaching services. Since the beginning of January I have been almost constantly in the inquiry-rooms and have seen from two to three hundred persons — perhaps four or five hundred — converted there. One great advantage gained by these meetings is that the pastor has an opportunity of becoming personally acquainted with young converts and inquirers; and it is no small thing to do that, because we will then be better prepared to give the right kind of instruction and counsel. As to the methods to be adopted for making these meetings a part of the services of our churches, I have adopted the plan of making the evening service, short, bringing it to a close by half-past eight. I refer to the evening service, because that is the time when the sermons are especially with a view to reaching the unconverted. As soon as the sermon is concluded, I send half a dozen persons down into the church parlors to sing; and half a dozen more to make themselves polite, and see that strangers are given an invitation to come in. It is most important that stiffness and formality should be abolished, and that all should get the idea that the inquiry-room is a place where the utmost friendliness and home-feeling is cultivated. In ten minutes after the meeting is begun we usually settle down to work, those who are unable to do anything else helping in the singing. About ten or twenty persons sit down to converse with the inquirers, and in this way five or six hundred souls have been brought to accept Christ. It is necessary, moreover, that the preaching should be of such a character as to awaken inquiry in order that these meetings should be successful. Strike while the iron is hot, but take care that the iron shall become hot by striking. Make your sermons full of Christ and his love, and of the great truths of the Gospel, and then you will always have inquirers seeking the way of salvation."

But there may be those who feel that they lack some of the peculiar qualifications that would fit them to enter into such a work, or there may be a prejudice in the church against the inquiry-meeting as a conclusion to the preaching service on Sunday evening, as to make the attempt injudicious; for the benefit of such we now present a second method:

Rev. D. Robert Boyd was in the habit of holding his inquiry-meeting on every Monday evening as a private and friendly religious conversation, either at his own house or at the church.

"During the many years," he writes in the introduction to a little tract that records some of the conversations at these meetings, "during the many years that God permitted me to occupy the responsible and delightful position of a Christian pastor, it was my habit to have a meeting for inquirers every Monday evening, both in summer and winter, in times of revival, and in times when there was no special religious interest. I found that this plan had many advantages. It led me to aim at the conversion of souls all the time, and to prepare my sermons with that object in view; while the impenitent in my congregation were led to feel that I was praying and looking for their conversion, that they ought to come to Christ at once, and that they need not wait for a series of special services, nor till large numbers were joining the church, to secure the salvation of their souls. Accordingly, the notice for this meeting was given out regularly from the pulpit the same as that of the weekly prayer-meeting. I was at pains to explain that the meeting was not to be confined to souls in an anxious state about their personal salvation, but was open to Christians who were in any perplexity about religious subjects, or anything that was disturbing their peace of mind, or hindering their growth in grace. Even persons troubled with sceptical doubts were urged to come and have a candid talk with me. The result was, I was seldom without inquirers, and the conversations on these occasions greatly helped me in preparations for the pulpit. They gave me something to aim at, of a definite character, and made my sermons more practical than they might otherwise have been."

"When Rev. George Mueller was in Chicago last year," writes Dr. Gray, in *The Interior*, "he stated in an address to the ministers of the city, 'that the eminent Robert Hall, during his ministry of eight years in Bristol, had not been instrumental in adding a single new convert to his church. This information he had from a very intelligent Christian lady, a great admirer of Mr. Hall, and a zealous member of his church, who greatly deplored the fact of this apparent want of success. And yet Robert Hall was himself a noble Christian, a faithful preacher of the Gospel, and the prince of pulpit orators of his time. Now what should we infer from a fact like this? Certainly we must not infer that Mr. Hall did not preach the truth. His life and whole published works would contradict any such conclusion. And most assuredly it would be a most superficial judgment to say that Mr. Hall did no good at Bristol because his preaching did not result in the actual conversion of souls. One plants and another waters; one sows and another reaps; God alone must give the increase. God sometimes withholds that increase through long years of patient, faithful toil. As for Robert Hall, he may have overshot the mark, and probably did, in his grand style of sermonizing. But we know that his masterly argumentation and splendid gifts of eloquence were not lost upon the church at large in the influence he exerted upon the leading minds of his generation, however they may seem to have been lost upon the sinners at Bristol. By his published sermons he still lives and preaches in many lands. In judging of the results, immediate or final, of any true preacher's work, we need always to bear in mind the caution given by the Master himself, 'Judge not according to the appearance; judge righteous judgment.'"

And yet it may be that ministers do not enough look and pray for immediate conviction and conversion to follow the preaching of their sermons. Thus Major Whittle told us in a series of meetings held here, that a Methodist minister in Cincinnati after preaching a Gospel sermon, was much surprised to find a man come forward and kneel before the pulpit.

"I thought," said the minister, "that he was drunk, and that I should have to get a police officer in order to avoid a disturbance. But instead of being drunk, the man was under conviction of sin, and came forward as an inquirer. And so I had been preaching Gospel truth, but without any expectation of immediate results. O how I was rebuked!"

And thus, whilst undoubtedly there are different lines of success in doing pastoral work, it may be true that we fail altogether to draw in the net as fishers of men. It may be that by means of an inquiry-meeting held either on Sabbath evening after the preaching services, or as a private meeting on some other evening of the week, the pastor shall so enlarge the work of the Sabbath, and the sphere of the prayer-meeting, as to make his ministry fruitful both in edifying the church, and in enlarging its membership by actual conversions. Let each, then, that is called to the work of the ministry earnestly and prayerfully seek out such methods of work as he can, with the blessing of God, most successfully prosecute.

CHAPTER VI.

Moody's Scripture Counsels for Inquirers.

Addressed to Christian Workers.

I HAVE chosen as my subject this morning, "How to hold an inquiry-meeting; or, what are the best adapted texts of Scripture to be dwelt upon at these meetings?" Of course I am not going to quote all the texts that could be used, and to good advantage; I am just going to bring to mind some of the best ones. And what I want first to call your attention to, if you are going to be successful in winning souls to Christ, is the need for discrimination in finding out people's differences. People are not the same in their wants, spiritual, more than temporal. What is good for one, is rank poison for another. You can't treat all alike. I've a friend that when he is sick always drinks a lot of hot water, and goes to bed. Another says to me, just take this dose and you will get well. It don't make any difference what's the matter with you, this friend has one single remedy. So many have just one verse of Scripture. He's always quoting it. It fits his case, and he thinks it does everybody else's. A man I know up in Wisconsin was converted under a railway bridge, and to this day he keeps urging people to go right down under that bridge, if they want to get converted sure. But God never repeats Himself. No two thoughts are just alike, no two needs are just alike, no two sinners are going to come to Christ in the same precise way. Instead of looking for others' experiences, look for one for yourself. So when talking to persons in the inquiry-room, you must find out just these differences. Now I am going to divide inquirers into classes, or divisions, this morning, and point out a few passages suitable for each.

The first class, I think, in point of numbers, is that of the doubters — those who are always in Doubting Castle. And these, generally, are among professing Christians. Oh, I think we shall make a different start with these, when we get to Boston, from what we did here. I'm convinced we made a mistake here in not opening the inquiry-rooms for professing Christians, first. For twenty or thirty years they have been living on, making empty professions. Now, they just want to get off their crutches, and get to walking and running for Christ. I don't believe they can accomplish much; I know they can't, if they continue in this half-dead state. If Christians haven't assurance, they are just stumbling blocks — they are in the way of the work. How many hurts these professing Christians give, who show no sign of their faith! They have no joy in serving the Lord, and their children with reason, say, "I don't want that kind of a religion." And here I want to call your attention to a proper remedy for this class, to be found in the Book of John. That whole book was written for this one thing, to help people out of Doubting Castle, and teach them that they may know they are saved. Only Friday last, I met a woman, a prominent member of a prominent church, who said it was presumption to say with certainty that we are saved. I said it was presumption to say that we are not saved, when we have the very word of the Lord Jesus Christ for it. Oh, if you will just read those precious words : "He that heareth my words and believeth on Him that sent me hath everlasting life, and shall not come into condemnation, but is passed from death unto life ;" and then turn to those other divine words : "These things have I written unto you that believe on the name of the Son of God, that ye may know that ye have eternal life, and that ye may believe on the name of the Son of God:" if you will just read these sure words of God, you will not talk about having no assurance as to your salvation. Just believe in the words of the Son of God, and you know right now that you are saved. You know right now, I say, and don't have to put it off till you are going to die. Therefore I would talk to these doubting citizens about the Epistle of John. I would say to you, persuade them to take these words of Jesus: "They have passed from death to life." Oh, yes, it is the privilege of every child of God, to know that he is saved.

The next class are the backsliding. They do not want so much assurance, as reviving. I know a lady who has a homœopathic doctor's book, and whenever she is at all out of sorts she goes right to it. In spiritual things there is a good remedy for all sorts, and for the backsliders as well. Though they have left God, He makes a way for them to return. I have just turned down the leaves of my Bible at the second and third chapters of Jeremiah. I don't think any one can feel this way with that Bible in hand. "Thus saith the Lord, what iniquity have your fathers found in me, that they are gone far from me, and have walked after vanity and are become vain?" Now, what did Christ ever do against you? Did He ever lie to you? Did He ever abuse you? Did He ever deceive you? Only one man ever said that, and he was out of his head, and any one would know he was. No man can accuse Christ of any bias or offence. "What iniquity have you found in me?" None at all. The trouble has been with ourselves. It was He that brought the early church through the wilderness, through all the dangers of the way, and into the promised land. It is He that gives you power and lifts you up. Oh say, then, what evil or iniquity have you found in Him? The trouble is with you, O backsliders, who "have forsaken the fountains of living water." The nineteenth verse says: "Thine own wickedness shall convict thee, and thy backslidings shall reprove thee; know therefore, and see that it is an evil thing and bitter that thou hast forsaken the Lord thy God, and that my fear is not in thee, saith the Lord of Hosts." Enforce the miseries of this text, and the use, the exhortation of the third chapter, twenty-second verse: "Return, ye backsliding children, and I will heal your backslidings. Behold we come unto thee; for thou art the Lord our God." And then, fourteenth verse: "Only acknowledge thine iniquity, that thou hast transgressed against the Lord thy God." I remember repeating these promises to a backslider, and he couldn't believe them at first for joy. How tender these words of Scripture to the backslider. Bring these words right to bear on them, and tell how God pleads with them. Read to them the opening words of Hosea, fourteenth chapter: "Return unto the Lord thy God, for thou hast fallen by thine iniquity; say unto him, take away all iniquity and receive us graciously. . . . . I (God) will heal their backsliding, I will love them freely; for mine anger is turned away." Then bring up the story of the prodigal for illustration; also the apostle Peter, how he was drawn to God after grievously backsliding, and how he was even admitted to the blessings of Pentecost. Then say, "You, too, can be restored if you only believe, and God will yet make you a blessing to believers."

The third class are those who are not stricken by their sins; who have no deep conviction of guilt. Just bring the law of God to bear on these, and show them themselves in their true light. Repeat Romans, third chapter, tenth verse: "There is none righteous, no, not one;" also the succeeding verses; and then repeat from Isaiah: "The whole head is sick, and the whole heart faint; from the sole of the foot even unto the head there is no soundness, but wounds and bruises and putrefying sores." And then bring in that verse, "The heart is deceitful above all things, and desperately wicked." Don't try to heal the wound before the hurt is felt. You may, perhaps, get but few satisfactory inquirers in this way, but what you do get are worth something. If a man don't see his guilt, he won't be a valuable or true convert. Read him the first chapter of First John, tenth verse: "If we say that we have not sinned, we make him a liar, and his word is not in us," and hold him right to it. Don't attempt to give the consolations of the Gospel until your converts see they have sinned — see it and feel it. I met a man who expressed doubts about his being much of a sinner.

"Well," said I, "let's find out if you have sinned. Do you swear?"

"Well, as a general rule, I only swear when I get mad."

"Yes, yes; but what does the Lord say about not holding a man guiltless that swears? Believe me, He will hold you responsible for that; bear that in mind; you must be able to hold your temper, but if not, beware to take the name of God in vain. Are you not now a sinner?"

And the man was convinced.

Sometimes, too, I have found a merchant this way; and yet one openly confesses to me that he did cheat sometimes.

"You lie, then, don't you?" said I. He didn't want to put it quite so plainly, but pretty soon saw it in my light. Oh, yes; enforce this truth kindly but firmly, that our natural hearts are as black and deceitful as hell. Man must say from his heart, "I have sinned and come short of the glory of God."

The fourth class are those completely broken down by a sense of sin, those who have too much conviction of sin, distinguished from the preceding inquirers, who haven't enough. One of these tells you that God can't save such a sinner as he. Then you have to prove his mistake, and show that God can save to the uttermost. Take the first chapter of Isaiah, eighteenth verse: "Come now, and let us reason together, saith the Lord; though your sins be as scarlet, they shall be white as snow; though they be red like crimson, they shall be as wool." Just turn your Bible right over to that passage, and many such other passages in Isaiah: they will all help in the inquiry room. The forty-third chapter, twenty-fifth verse says: "I, even I, am he that blotteth out thy transgressions for mine own sake, and will not remember thy sins." And the twenty-second verse of the next chapter is stronger: "I have blotted out, as a thick cloud, thy sins; return unto me, for I have redeemed thee." Make the anxious soul believe that God has blotted out his sins as a thick cloud; make him see the dense cloud vanishing, as it were, from the face of the sun, vanishing forever; that cloud can never come up again; others may, but that old cloud of the past guilt is dissolved forever; the Lord Himself has blotted it out. Use the two verses, John 1: 11, 12: "He came unto his own, and his own received him not. But as many as received him, to them gave he power to become the sons of God, even to them that believe on his name."

The idea is, that those fearing ones cannot serve God until they receive Christ fully as their salvation; it won't do for them to merely take up with some minister, or church, or creed. The minister dies or moves away; the only lasting resource is in Christ, at the right hand of God, where He will never forsake His own. Yes, press Jesus upon these anxious souls. Tell them " God so loved the world that he gave his only begotten son "—" so loved the world "— that includes them; if they inhabited some other land they might tremble, but they are on this earth, for all the sons and daughters of which Christ died, the just for the unjust. Use also the text: " Verily, verily, I say unto you, he that heareth my words, and believeth on him that sent me, shall not come into condemnation, but has passed from death unto life."

Now, some people do not just understand believing in Christ. They believe Christ came as an historical being, as Moses and Elijah came. They believe the Cunard line of steamers will take them to Liverpool in twelve or fourteen days. But these beliefs don't make men good; they are head beliefs only. They are not what your inquirers want. What you and they want is heart belief, or, in other words, to just trust Christ to save you. Sometimes people can't digest the word "belief;" then let them take this sweet word "trust." From Isaiah xxvi: 3, 4, read to them: "Thou wilt keep him in perfect peace whose mind is stayed on thee; because he trusteth in thee. Trust ye in the Lord forever; for in the Lord Jehovah is everlasting strength."

By trusting in Him, you see we have everlasting strength. You must get them to trust and believe entirely in Christ, and not try to save themselves. They cannot save themselves by their feelings; assure them of that. There is not a word of warrant for such a thought from the first of Genesis to the last of Revelation. Oh, it is much better to trust in the precious, changeless word of God, than in our own changing feelings; thank God, that this is also our duty!

Then you hear some inquirers say, "I haven't got strength sufficient." But Christ died to be their strength. A loving hand will support them in the Christian journey, and His strength will be made perfect in weakness. Bid such "be strong in the Lord, and in the power of His might."

And then another class that cannot be saved in this way, they think, because doubting instantaneous conversion. Read to such from Romans, the sixth chapter, twenty-third verse: "The wages of sin is death, but the gift of God is eternal life." Salvation is a gift, and so must have a definite point in time. I say, "Will you take this Bible?" You must first make up your mind to take it, and then reach out and — the work of an instant — grasp the gift. Just so with God's best gift, salvation; to take it is the work of an instant, and your inquirer may have it for the asking. "Let him that heareth say come;" "Whosoever will, let him come and drink of the water of life freely." With the gift, God gives the power to take it. When we get before the tribunal of the great white throne, we will have to answer for it, if we refuse to take it. This is the richest jewel that heaven has; God gives up His Son for our Saviour.

Another class say to you and me when, in the inquiry-room, we press them to openly confess Christ, "We're afraid we won't hold out." Say to these repeatedly that blessed text: "Now unto him that is able to keep you from falling." Think, and tell them to think of the thousands who never fall. The idea that it is necessary to fall into sin is wrong. Then take those passages: "I, the Lord thy God, will hold thy right hand"; "Fear not, I will help thee," and "I am persuaded that he is able to keep that which I have committed unto him against that day." Let a man just trust the Lord to keep him from falling, and He will do it.

Suppose I have a hundred thousand dollars with me; it's all I have in the world; thieves are after it, and I'm quaking every minute lest they get it. I find my banker here, and I say, "Here, take it quick; I can't keep my money but by your help; I wish you would hurry and put it in the vault; when it is deposited there, and not before, I shall be safe."

Is not this the way to give our all into God's keeping? Is not this the way to live secure from temptation and backsliding? In God's keeping we are safe. "Our life is hid with Christ in God." Oh, let us each make this deposit of our personal trust this morning; trust him entirely, and then we can the better lead inquirers in the same way. Jesus can hold us close to Himself. "Nor height, nor depth, nor any other creature shall be able to separate us from the love of God, which is in Christ Jesus our Lord." If you just take up the words of Christ in the book of Romans, love and peace and joy flow out. One verse tells of love, and the next of joy; the next and next, of the peace that comes from believing. Romans, fourth chapter and twenty-eighth verse, and all those verses a'ong there might be read. The result of believing is joy, rest, and peace. John xv : 11, that is joy. Matt. xi : 28, that is rest. John xiv : 27, that is peace. Never, however, tell a man he is converted. Never tell him he is saved. Let him find that out from heaven. You can't afford to deceive one about this great question. But you can help his faith and trust, and lead him right.

I find that those in the inquiry-room do best who do not run about from one to another, offering words of encouragement everywhere. They would better go to but one or two of an afternoon or evening. We are building for eternity and can take time. The work will not then be superficial. If it is so, it will not be the fault of the workers or preachers. And then, to do all our duty, we must talk more of restitution. I don't think we preach enough the need of our making good to one another injuries to person, property, or feeling. If you have done one a detriment, you must go and pay it back, or make it up, if it is a tangible loss, and if it is a wound to the feelings, fully apologize. It is a good deal better to go up and do the fair thing, whatever the result. It may be that some will refuse such amends, but it is our duty to offer them. But in the end a complete reconciliation from such a course is almost sure to result. The antipathy supposed to exist on the other side is often only imagined. You need not expect that God is going to forgive you if you don't forgive others. We say daily, "Forgive us our debts as we forgive our debtors," and we must show that we understand this conditional request. What if God should take us at our word, and just forgive us to the extent to which our small grievances are forgiven! And this He surely will do; so let us be wise.

A young lady in Michigan, at a recent revival service, was troubled greatly, and to kind inquiries at last confessed that her unwillingness to confess Christ resulted from a school-room quarrel which was still unsettled. She felt she couldn't forgive her enemy, but at last told her trouble and asked for advice. "Must I forgive my mate?" "Certainly, if you want God's forgiveness," was the answer of the minister, and immediately she ran with all her might to her old friend, and instead of meeting a cold reception they were soon crying on each others necks.

And so it always should be, and most always there will be, the same prompt half-way meeting between those aggrieved. My wife was laboring in the inquiry-room the other evening with a lady who was in just this state of mind, and very soon separation and complete reconciliation were effected, and two old friends walked off arm in arm, happier than ever before this little misunderstanding. And one of those ladies felt so strong in her new-found charity for all, that she won over her husband, and last Sunday he openly in the Tabernacle confessed Christ, remembering that "with the mouth confession is made unto salvation." Many more texts, did time allow, might be cited, all applicable to anxious inquirers.

But one word more. Do not let a man go out of the inquiry-room without praying with him. Fear not, but do the work boldly. There was a man the other day who said, "I don't believe there's any God." The resolute Christian worker, to whom he spoke, answered impetuously, "I will just ask God to shake you — to just shake this demon out of you." And down he fell on his knees by the poor infidel and prayed with loud earnestness. The man began to shake from head to foot. It was God shaking him. And by just these means, more than any others, skeptics and infidels will know there is a God. Let me say a word to those ministers that have not, and do not go into the inquiry room. Many in your flocks, never seeing you there, think you are not in sympathy with this work, and they begin to think you don't care anything about their salvation. They feel in bondage, and you do not go to help them. Well, there was a minister in a city we visited, who did not "condescend" to be seen in our humble Tabernacle. He would have nothing to do with us. One day he was at a dinner-party where they were discussing our work. Said he:

"That sort of a thing is good enough for those people, but it would never do for me."

"Well," said another clergyman of the same belief, "fifty-seven of your congregation stood up in the Tabernacle for prayers to-day, and all of them afterward went into the inquiry-room."

The cultured and popular pastor of those Christians could not kill the humane promptings to be charitable to all professing the name of Christ, and to worship along with such, even in perhaps irregular modes. But with the cordial co-operation of every pastor in the Tabernacle and inquiry-room, what limit would there be to the Christian inroads on the citadels of sin? Oh, make it a duty, all of you, to talk to some soul at every meeting, in these blessed inquiry-rooms. Don't take those in a position in life above your own, but take those on the same footing. Bend all your endeavors to answer for poor, struggling souls that question of all importance to them, "What must I do to be saved?" Yes, this is the question. What else, but to answer it, brought out these thousands at this early hour? My friends, God is with you in this work. Go on more diligently and implicitly, trusting in him; go on to a more and more glorious harvest.

CHAPTER VII.

THE VALUE OF TOPICS.

A FEW reasons may be given to show the value of topics in keeping up an interest in prayer-meetings. And the advantages, it seems to me, so largely overbalance the disadvantages as to very generally recommend their use.

Where the subjects are selected for a whole year in advance, or for parts of a year, the pastor will take in a wider range of Christ-life, doctrine and experience, than if waiting to the day of the meeting, and then making, as is so often the case, a hasty selection.

But the great advantage is, that it enables the people to prepare their minds with reference to a given subject. Where no topic has been announced, the people have had no opportunity to consider it, and look up passages of Scripture to illustrate its meaning and enforce its teaching. Does it not seem a little unfair, or ironical, after a leader has about exhausted the subject in a long address, to say, "Now, brethren, the meeting is open. Do not let precious time slip by in waiting for each other." If the people have equal opportunities for preparation with the leader, there is less liability that the prayer-meeting shall become a one-man meeting. Thus at a certain prayer-meeting, as I have been informed, the minister delivered a long lecture on hell, which consumed nearly the whole time. If the leader does not claim that he chooses his subject on the instant by inspiration, and talks by inspiration, then the subject of the evening admits of choice before the opening; and if it admits of previous choice, there is no good reason why the knowledge of it shall be withheld from the people, and they not permitted to benefit themselves by it. If a meeting is not profitable to which the leader comes without any preparation, is it not an advantage to the meeting, to have all, both pastor and people, come to it with due preparation and prayer? If it be said, "We cannot tell so long in advance what special spiritual needs may arise each week to demand attention," the answer is, whenever such special emergencies arise as do not seem to have been provided for in a comprehensive plan of selection from Scripture texts for a given time, discard the set topic, and introduce the new one, with due notice of the change.

The use of topics, also will secure the advantages of associated Bible study. The thought of the church will be concentrated upon the same subject during a given week, that will secure unity on the subject, and a rich variety in its presentation. There is almost an endless variety by which to illustrate the subject, both by anecdote and experience, and inasmuch as no two minds are exactly alike, each one will come with some new thought and illustration that will prove stimulating and interesting. Suppose the subject to be, "Christ the Light of the World." One speaker may be led to present the physical analogies of the sun, as the source of light, heat and chemical power, and then pass from that to consider the moral condition of the heathen world without the light of the Sun of Righteousness. Another speaker may be led to present Christ as the light of the world that reveals the Father; that fills it with the warmth of divine love, and becomes the source of all holy and heavenly activities. Another may present the duty of preaching the Gospel to the heathen, as shown by those contrasts of light and darkness. And another, finally, may dwell upon those passages of Scripture which present Christ as the light of heaven. He is the light of the present world, and He will also be the light of the world to come.

In this way the prayer-meeting will become not merely a training-school for the gifts and graces of the church, but also a school for the attractive presentation of Scripture truth. And by such helps as are generally derived from associated study, the prayer-meeting will be kept from running into "ruts and set phrases," which must eventually become old and tiresome. Bishop Simpson said to a friend with whom he was walking home from a religious service:

"That was a beautiful prayer we heard?"

"Yes," replied the man, "it was so; but I have heard it for the last twenty years."

The minister is apt to look at a question from a theoretical and philosophical standpoint; but if the people have equal opportunities for preparation and are trained to take a part, they will counteract this tendency, and present the practical bearings of a subject as illustrated from the standpoint of daily life, business cares, household duties, peculiar temptations, vexations and cares.

CHAPTER VIII.

OBJECTIONS TO THEIR USE.

WE see a thing more clearly when we look at it from all sides. There are some who object to the use of topics, for one reason and another; and I may say as an introduction to a statement of some of these that I have never attended a prayer-meeting of the kind to be described. I have never attended one which was not seriously conducted and solemnly participated in; I have never attended a prayer-meeting that degenerated into a debating society, or into a school for the display of oratory; but I have heard of prayer-meetings so "spontaneous and fresh" that no one has spoken a word save the pastor, who oft and again after having had his say, would dismiss the people before the hour was half up.

"I rise to say," writes the Rev. Donald Fletcher, in an article contributed to the *Interior*, last year, "that you cannot have a good prayer-meeting when you announce a topic ahead. The trouble is the men get to studying up speeches, and if there is anything more rasping than that I don't know of it. You go to meeting Wednesday night for your spiritual luncheon in the middle of the week, tired, thirsty, hungry for the Bread and Water of Life. The topic announced, ' Is Christianity in danger !' The leader shows that it is not. Twenty minutes gone. A hymn is sung slowly to get the full benefit of it; then a long pause, for the leader has said the meeting is open, and, like the Clark street bridge, it stays open quite a while. After looking sheepishly around at each other, and moving nervously in their seats, the people see Bro. A rise up slowly stroking his beard, and that twinkle in the left eye, raised a little higher than the other, shows that he is prepared to make a 'few remarks.' And at it he goes — not even Spencer or dead Stuart Mill left out. Ten, twelve, but the coughing and leaf-turning fetch him down on the thirteenth minute. He lately bought Joseph Cook's Biology. Then the hymn, 'Hallelujah! 'tis done.' Then a man who once made Fourth of July speeches, and prides himself in saying that he is naturally of a skeptical turn of mind, proceeds after taking exception to 'Just one remark the brother has made, though he agrees substantially with him,' he keeps the floor to ventilate his new cyclopedia, and seems to make the impression that it is very kind in him not to turn infidel as he closes with an eulogy on 'the greatest elevating and civilizing power that we know of, my friends, in the annals of ancient or modern history.' By this time it is nine o'clock, for appearance sake though, the prayer-meeting must have a second prayer, then 'Pull for the shore' is sung, then 'Bolt for the door' is done. Thus endeth that communion of saints. A topic announced on Sunday destroys spontaneous enthusiasm and freshness in those that speak; begets a critical spirit in those that listen; robs you of a prayer and conference meeting; leaves you a very poor lyceum, and starves those who want heart religion. The noon prayer-meeting in Chicago is not half as good as it was five years ago, for no other reason, I believe, than that they carry out the programme of subjects drawn up by the International Committee. Why 'Faith' and the 'Atonement' are announced only two or three times a year! And there are from twenty to fifty unconverted strangers present every day, but the man who drew up the subjects could not, like Shakespeare 'repeat himself.' Which leads me to say that I never knew of a good prayer-meeting where there was not a reaching out after the unconverted. God will not encourage selfishness that 'wants a blessing' if it is just to 'enjoy a good meeting.' May I suggest then to pastors: Make your prayer-meeting a feeder for your next Sunday sermon. You got your subject Monday morning, of course. You toss it up like a ball, think it up, read it up all the week, and crystalize it Friday. Your opening remarks on Wednesday evening should be in the direction or neighborhood of your next Sunday's subject. Your thoughts are all fresh. You will strike fire first sentence; people will spring to their feet all through the hour, especially if you quietly by yourself request one or two of your people each week to fill the first five-second pause that occurs, which is usually after the meeting is thrown open. No two churches are alike in their states and characteristics. The Lord alone can direct the pastor to the subject he should have for the pulpit and prayer-meeting. And it is not 'give us this year our yearly bread.' We get it as we need it. How well Mr Muller, of Bristol, put it when asked how he got his sermons. 'I ask the Lord to direct me and when a subject comes to my mind and my soul is at rest within me, I conclude, that is the one the Lord gives me.' What our prayer-meetings need is, not uniformity, but informality, less stiffness, more homelikeness. Given an impromptu, fervent, quick prayer-meeting, and you find a good preacher, a happy pastor and people. Given a cut and dried yawnish prayer-meeting, and there you find unrest, gossip, barrenness, and from such, good Lord deliver us."

It seems to me that a general verdict has already been prononunced upon these "spontaneous" meetings by the church membership, as may be inferred from the fact that so very few — a number discouragingly small — attend them, and that the faithful pastor has to sustain nearly all the parts himself in the meeting. The question, is a fair one. Has Brother Fletcher ever conducted a prayer-meeting in a provincial town, or in the country regularly for a number of years, and if so will he be kind enough to give the results of such an experience?

CHAPTER IX.

OBJECTIONS CONSIDERED.

AND now, having presented, as in the preceding chapter, some objections to the use of topics in the prayer-meeting, it may not be out of place to introduce the reply which this article called out, and which was published in the same paper a week or two following. Both of these articles, of course, were written in the utmost good humor, and the spice and flavor with which they abound only serve to make their reading more enjoyable.

"As I was walking home from the office with the *Interior* of the 5th inst.," writes the Rev. A. Emery Fisher, of Mineral Point, Wis., "the first words that caught my eye were, 'I rise to say that you cannot have a good prayer-meeting when you announce a topic ahead.'

"Now, is this true? Do the facts in the case warrant such a sweeping, unqualified assertion? If they do, then how woefully I have been deceived in many of my topical prayer-meetings. I recognize the objection 'studying up speeches.' Practically, it does not exist.

There are no speeches made in our average prayer-meeting. Ministers know, painfully, how difficult it is to induce persons to take any part, other than prayer; and if this desired end can be secured by having a topic announced, let them be proclaimed from every pulpit of the land. And if it is desirable to have words at all, let them be studied words, studied in the proper sense, by meditation and by prayer. The article in question states further:

"'A topic announced on Sunday, destroys spontaneous enthusiasm and freshness in those that speak.'

"Now that sounds nicely. It is pretty. It is attractive. But it is only a bubble. Puncture it and it will collapse. It is nothing but wind enveloped in a gaudy covering of words. (1.) If it be necessary for 'enthusiasm and freshness' in the prayer-meeting to keep its members ignorant of the topic for the evening, why would it not be well in the pulpit to keep the minister ignorant of his subject till it is time for him to speak? If it be well on Wednesday evening, why would it not be well on Sabbath morning? I acknowledge that the two cases are not quite parallel. (2.) If it does not destroy 'enthusiasm and freshness' for the pastor to meditate upon a subject, and 'toss it up like a ball' before he speaks upon it, why should it produce in an elder, a deacon, or one of the rank and file barrenness and drouth? (3.) 'Spontaneous enthusiasm' is not the object for which God's people assemble for prayer. It is to commune with our heavenly Father; to receive the blessing of the Holy Spirit; to eat of the bread from our own Master's table; to be 'strengthened with might, by His spirit in the inner man.' You may have a meeting full of 'enthusiasm and freshness' from beginning to end and yet go away as sterile and and weak as you came. I do not deprecate these elements in our meeting, but when they are made the chief good of our coming together, the husks are chosen instead of the manna, the waters of Albana instead of the Jordan, the flourish of trumpets instead of the 'still small voice singing in silence.'

"The next paragraph has the right ring. His advice to pastors is good. But it tramples in the dust all that has gone before. The suggestion is for them to take the topic for the next Sabbath's discourse, which has been selected on Monday, for the subject of the prayer-meeting. 'Your thoughts are all fresh. You will strike fire the first sentence.' Do not be too sure of it. I have seen some flint-locks if you got fire from them the third or fourth pull you would do pretty well. But look at it in relation to the foregoing part of this article. If the pastor, by having the topic before his mind from Monday till the meeting for prayer, comes with freshness and vivacity of thought, why should not others? Why contemplating a topic secures freshness in the pastor and dryness in others, I cannot quite comprehend. Mr. Fletcher is right when he affirms, that by study and prayer the best thoughts are secured, and therefore I rise to say:

"You can have a good prayer-meeting when the topic is announced ahead. But now to the Law and the Prophets. It seems to me we have some Scriptural example, if not authority, for topical prayer-meetings. Christ says: 'If two of you agree on earth as touching any thing they shall ask, etc.' What ever two or more persons may agree upon to pray for, is the topic for that meeting. Again: When Christ saw the greatness of the harvest and the fewness of the reapers, He announces a topical prayer-meeting: 'Pray ye, therefore, the Lord of the harvest, that He will send forth laborers into the harvest.' Here the topic was previously announced, and I presume they had a good prayer-meeting. Let us not condemn what Christ commends. There is another. The prayer-meeting at Pentecost was a topical one, and Christ himself announced it. It was: 'The Baptism of the Holy Ghost.' I do not know whether they 'studied up speeches' or not, or whether it was void of 'spontaneous enthusiasm and freshness,' but I do know that it was a blessed meeting, for they received power from on high. Should not this not only hush our opposition but awaken our hearts to favor when we know that the Apostolic Church had its origin in a prayer-meeting at which a topic was previously announced. But there is one more. Peter is in prison. The church holds a topical prayer-meeting. I do not think it was announced the Sunday before. But they have but one topic before them, viz.— Peter's Deliverance — and it was an ever memorable occasion, for Peter stood knocking at the gate. Will the brother call that a good meeting?

"But historically: In the history of the church, the great impulses to a revival of religion have had their birth in meetings for prayer, where they have come together with one accord and one topic. All the revivals in which I have been concerned can be traced to the unity of hearts for the one great thing. And my meetings which have been the richest in heavenly blessings, where it seemed 'that God came down our souls to greet,' have been those where I announced the topic from the pulpit on Sabbath morning. Has not the Week of Prayer been a great blessing to the church? Yet they are topical meetings. All the objections that the zealous brother urges lie not against the announcing the topic, but at the door of those who 'study up speeches' as delineated in the article in question.

"This is most clearly set forth in the *Interior* of the 12th inst., in Mrs. C. M. Livingston's report of her prayer-meeting. What a vast difference between her's and Mr. Fletcher's. Both were topical, and previously announced, but they are as diverse as two worlds. Who will say the last was not a good and blessed meeting. Yes, you can have the presence of God when you have the topic announced."

CHAPTER X.

SOME OPINIONS OF PASTORS.

On the Utility of Topics.

THE use of subjects for the prayer-meeting, previously announced for the benefit of the people, either by printed card or by word of mouth from the pulpit, is no longer a matter of speculation merely, but has received the test of trial for years past, by hundreds and thousands of churches in all parts of the land, and, so far as is known to me, has resulted in the decided improvement of prayer-meetings, both in the matter of attendance, and in an increase in the number of those who take part in the exercises. I have thought the opinions of pastors who have subjected this thing to trial would present our subject in the light, and with the force which experience gives to theory.

The following remarks on the utility of topics by some of my brethren in the ministry, which have been so kindly placed at my disposal, are very interesting, and enforce themselves :

224 E. 12th St., New York, April 7th, 1879.

Rev. Lewis O. Thompson, Peoria, Ill.:

My dear Brother — For several years past, here and in my former charge at Toronto, in Canada, I have used a prepared list of topics in the prayer-meeting, and this experience is altogether in favor of such a plan.

1. It saves the leader from the harassing and often humiliating hunt for a subject, from week to week, sometimes at the last moment.

2. It renders possible a systematic consideration of related subjects, grouped in short courses, covering a few weeks.

3. It enables the brethren of the church who take part in the service, to come with that preparation which enables them to do so with the best effect; for which purpose the leader can bespeak their assistance beforehand.

4. Special provision can be systematically made for adopting the topics to the several seasons of the year, and for taking up missionary fields, temperance, and such special interests.

5. If it is desired to have the prayer-meeting follow up the teaching of the Sunday-school or of the pulpit, the topics can be arranged accordingly.

6. The experience of other brethren, in the selection and arrangement of topics, can be made use of by any pastor in relation to his own meeting.

7. The same benefits that accrue from union in a common course of S. S. Lessons are made possible as to the prayer-meeting, when the churches of a city or district agree on a common list. The topic of the week becomes a matter of general study and conversation. Any prayer-meeting attendant is at home, if he "drops in" at such a service away from his own place. Perhaps, already, the religious papers publish "Prayer-meeting Helps." If not, they may.

8. The possible objection, that meetings may become "cut and dry," is not realized in fact. If the topics are spicy in themselves, and are handled by live men, this will not be. Some of the driest services I have known, have been on the extempore plan.

9. Should any special state of feeling arise, necessitating a departure from the printed plan, no sensible leader would hesitate a moment to lay it aside for one or more meetings. But this will not happen so often as might be apprehended.

10. The experience of the churches and Y. M. C. Associations who have *tried this plan*, is strongly in favor of it. F. H. MARLING,
Pastor 14th St. Presby. Ch.

Rock Island, Ill., April 14th, 1879.

My dear Brother—On the matter of "Topics for the Prayer-meeting," I would say that all through my ministry, it has been my custom, in some way, to have the people know in advance what the subject would be. Sometimes I have announced the topic from week to week, and sometimes by printed list. But my preference is for the latter method, for several reasons. The subjects can be carefully selected, as is not always the case when they are chosen and announced from meeting to meeting. Subjects properly related to each other, and in their proper and natural order, can thus be brought to the attention of the people. Thus, with care on the part of the pastor, or committee, selecting topics, the themes for the year can be made to form a concatenated series of profitable studies and meditations. In preparing the course for the whole year, opportunity is also given for a large variety of subjects, avoiding the narrow range of easy and familiar topics, to which many of us are so apt to turn for prayer-meetings. All of these points place, as it will be observed, great responsibility on the person or persons selecting and arranging the list for the year.

Then there are other advantages quite as great. The people all know what the subject is to be, and, if they are diligent, can come to the meeting with hearts full of it, ready to understand and enjoy what is said, even if they take no part themselves. Those who are accustomed to speak, can come prepared to speak to the point, and not to wander aimlessly in unpremeditated speech. Thus unity will be given to the meetings, and they will not fall into fragments like one which I attended some time ago, when the pastor spoke on the parable of the leaven, an elder following on the observance of the Sabbath, another on the importance of family training, a third on the love of God, and an enthusiastic young brother, only a few weeks a Christian, fervently pleading with the members, every one a professing Christian, to come to Jesus.

    Fraternally yours,

        J. R. MILLER.
    Pastor Broadway Presby. Ch.

"This is the third year," writes Rev. S. C. Palmer, of Lockland, Ohio, "that I have been using prepared topics in my mid-week prayer-meetings, and I unhesitatingly give my testimony in favor of them. They have been very helpful to me, in that I have a subject always ready. They add much to the interest of our meetings, the brethren who study them being ready with some thought in harmony with the subject — the sisters also adding their help by way of parallel Scripture, either recited or read.

"Sometimes a subject seems bare when we first take it up, but study, and a comparison of ideas, always bring rich fruit. To us it is also a pleasant thought to remember that many others of our brethren elsewhere are engaged in the study of the same passage at the same time.

"My private opinion is, that this whole subject of prayer-meeting topics is yet in its infancy.

"I predict that the day is near when all Christian people will be engaged at the same time, upon the same passage, in their prayer-meetings, and that our religious papers will employ the best talent to prepare each week an article for aiding the general reader in getting ready for the prayer-meeting.

"If that time comes, of course we shall have an abundance of literature upon the subject. My opinion is that very much good might now be done, if our religious papers would establish a prayer-meeting department, and invite the pastors of our churches to contribute their plans and methods.

"My *heart* is in the *improvement* of the *prayer-meeting.*"   Fraternally, etc.

S. C. PALMER.
Pastor, Lockland, Ohio.

Experience has been long considered a good teacher

The writer has learned in this school that "topics for the prayer-meeting" are useful both to pastor and people. It saves the pastor many a precious moment' looking for the right passage, or subject, for the next meeting.

It gives the people an opportunity to know in advance the theme for the evening, and to make some preparation, if disposed, for participating in the services.

It tends to secure system in the weekly instructions, which is one of the essentials to growth in grace.

The past year, which is the first in which I have used printed topics, has been the most satisfactory one of my ministry in this department; and I do not hesitate to commend the plan heartily to those who have not tried it.

J. D. KERR.
Pastor 17th St. Presby. Ch., Denver, Col.

ATTLEBORO' FALLS, MASS., April 7th, 1879.

Bro. Thompson — I can *cordially* respond to your request, for in my experience I have found the giving out of "topics" to be remarkably efficient. Those who wish to flood a meeting with "experience" which is no experience, and with "testimonies" which, as they give them, are often worse than total silence, object on the ground that topics narrow the range and hamper their freedom. But I have thought the topics good on this very ground.

I have also found my people willing to give some preparation to the prayer-meeting when they knew the topic. God bless you for your labor of love in the grand prayer-meeting work, which draws more on my nervous system than my pulpit labors.

Yours truly,
F. D. KELSEY.

Topics, selected and announced beforehand, are useful in promoting and increasing the interest in the prayer-meeting in several ways. There is a degree of curiosity in every individual, and this is awakened and becomes alert when a topic for discussion is announced. The curious ones will come, then, to hear what the pastor or others may have to say on this subject, and the Spirit of the Lord may direct the word of power and salvation to their souls. The thoughtful ones will meditate and ponder over the topic, until they become so interested that they will speak to others, and thus the interest will grow and widen, and when the time for prayer-meeting comes, there will be several persons "full of the subject." The reading ones will run through their books and papers to find something bearing on the topic, and thus will bring their minds into the right channel, and come to the meeting with freshened ideas and new zeal. The praying ones will have a subject upon which to frame their prayers, and in this way will easily get out of the "old ruts" and "set phrases," and come to the house of prayer with an entirely new stock of feelings. The singing ones will select their songs and key their voices in adaptation to the topic, and thus the music will be with the "understanding" as well as "with the spirit." Above all, by announcing the topic, the pastor has committed himself to the study of the subject, and then, by the help of the Spirit, its elaboration will be for the profit of all.

C. W. CARTER.
Pastor M. E. Ch. Bastrop, La.

DETROIT, April 24th, 1879.

My dear Brother—What I deem of the highest importance is the furnishing the members of the church with a printed scheme of topics, so that they may know beforehand the subject to be talked and prayed about. Those who take part in the meeting will thus come prepared to speak, and all will take far more interest in the conference than they otherwise could. We would on no account abandon the plan of prayer-meeting schemes.

Truly yours,
Geo. D. Baker, D. D.

Rev. L. O. Thompson:

Deposit, N. Y., April 14th, 1879.

Dear Brother — About two years and a half ago, I introduced such a series of topics in the prayer-meeting, printing a few slips for distribution from month to month, on a little hand-press I have. On doing so, there was, to my mind, an evident increase of interest on the part of those attending, and much more point in the prayers and remarks of those taking part in the meeting. This plan was followed through the last year and a half of my last pastorate. To show how it was liked by the membership, I have only to say, that though vacant for nearly a year, they kept up their meetings in the same way, sending to me for a list of subjects, and I believe are pursuing the same plan to-day.

I came to this place last May, and at once proposed and put in operation the list of topics, and I am satisfied that the meetings have increased both in numbers and interest, and that those attending are generally pleased, and I trust edified.

From this experience then, I am prepared to say that the plan is a good one, and works well. My methods of conducting, I vary. One week it will be a Bible-reading; another, I will divide up the topic or passage of Scripture into parts, or subjects, or questions, and ask three, four, or five each to talk on one which I assign them; or I sometimes leave the meeting to their spontaneous thought on the subject. Thus I try to have variety as well as unity in my meetings.

I remain yours fraternally,

JAS. B. FISHER,
Pastor, Deposit, N. Y.

OWATONNA, MINN., April 15th, 1879.

REV. L. O. THOMPSON :

Dear Brother— I have been using the topical system in my prayer-meetings since the beginning of the present year. While this is not, perhaps, a sufficient length of time in which thoroughly to test the system, yet I am convinced from my brief experience that the plan is an admirable one, and that if faithfully followed it would invariably result in awakening a deeper interest in the meetings of our churches for prayer and the study of the Word. With us the plan is working well, and I am sure the same will prove true of any other church, if care is exercised in the selection and arrangement of the topics. Fraternally,

C. H. DeWolfe.
Pastor Baptist Ch.

CHAPTER XI.

SOME VIEWS OF MINISTERS.

On the Advantages to be Derived from Using Uniform Subjects.

THERE is, at the present time, a marked tendency in the direction of a number of churches, uniting to use the same topics for their prayer-meetings. There are as many as five or six series of lists being used in concert by as many different clusters of Christians in their circles of prayer, and I know not how many others there may be, who are associated for the same purpose. If subjects should be made uniform for all Christian churches, we should secure still more thought, preparation, prayer and exposition for them. Religious papers would then be willing to devote a portion of their space for hints and methods to increase the efficiency of this branch of the church's work. The persons having the greatest wisdom, skill and experience would be chosen for the annual committee to select a list of topics for each year to cover the various ranges of Christian experience, fellowship, communion and relative duties to God and to fellow-man, as these find illustration and enforcement in the Word of God and are "profitable for doctrine, for reproof, for correction, for instruction in righteousness; that the man of God may be perfect, thoroughly furnished unto all good works."

Such a custom may prove useful in drawing Christian denominations still nearer to each other. All the fruit that the International series of S. S. lessons has been bearing, will be borne by uniform Scriptural topics for the prayer-meeting. There is not that bitterness manifest between sects and denominations that formerly existed. Uniform texts of Scripture for circles of prayer would prove a standing evangelical alliance, and draw Christian hearts nearer to God and nearer to each other. To pray over the same subjects from the Bible, on each recurring prayer-meeting night throughout the year, would bear a harvest of fraternity, sweetness and love. It would also prove of great help to churches without pastors and stated supplies.

It gives me pleasure to be able to introduce some views of the clergy on advantages to be derived from using the same subjects for the weekly prayer-meeting. The first article was written by the Rev. J. C. McClintock, and presents the whole matter in a clear and philosophic light that must secure for this chapter a greater share of public attention than I could hope to secure in any other way. This article was first printed in the *Herald and Presbyter* of Cincinnati:

"Some people," he writes, "are born full of objections. They are ready with a protest against the nurse's first handling, and all subsequent experiences find them in the same mood. Irish fashion, they are bound always to see the other side of anything offered them first; and one of the surest ways to win them, is to oppose them. But, after all, they are a most vigorous and valuable element in society. I used to be out of patience with their ways — always pointing out the weak spots in the plan, and seeing the dangers in the way, and cooling off the ardor of thoughtless enthusiasts. But I confess now to a growing respect and sympathy for the constitutional and chronic objector. It is a good plan to look at the *other side* before leaping into any new project. So I have tried to look up some of the objections that are sure to be made against the idea of uniform topics for the prayer-meeting, and to question these objections by the facts of experience:

"1. The proposed plan of uniform topics can not meet the wants of the individual churches. No committee can know the condition of all the churches, and what might suit one would not suit another.

"The same objection was made against the idea of uniform topics for the Sunday-schools, and it was carried further. They said the classes of the same school can not be united in the study of the same lesson. But experience shows they can. You recall Mr. McCook's answer to this objection: 'The joint that would make a good roast for the adults would also make a nourishing broth for the children.' It depends on the cooking, you see. If the topics of the prayer-meeting cover the ordinary range of subjects, practical, experimental and doctrinal, that are needed in an average church they will be very likely to suit exactly the church at large. God's word has a wonderful adaptability to the experiences and wants of men and women everywhere. God's promise, 'I will help thee,' may come with equal force and comfort to the poor tired seamstress who is almost broken down by the drudgery of her life, and who has come to the prayer-meeting for encouragement; and to the business man who has the perplexities of a trade worth a million dollars tormenting his brain.

"2. This plan allows no opportunity to take advantage of passing events, or the providential circumstances of the pastor and people. The topic for the evening may find some congregation in the house of Bochim. It is true that sometimes the passage of Scripture, in course, may not be what the pastor would have selected to meet the circumstances of his people. In such exceptional cases let him depart from the regular course. Just as we do in Sunday-school. But this departure will not be called for very often. So full of truth is God's Word, and so flexible is it, that there are few passages or chapters that may not be so applied as to meet the present wants of the people. Most of the Word can be read in the light of to-day's trials or duties.

"3. This plan would interfere with the liberty of the pastors in their peculiar province. It would interrupt their plans of work. Most pastors could lay out a course of study and plan a set of prayer-meeting topics for their own people, that would be better adapted to them than any that a committee could furnish.

"This is all true — probably. But, as a matter of facts, few pastors or churches have a regular plan of work for the prayer-meeting. Many pastors give but little time to the study of the prayer-meeting topic, and often there is no topic selected until the pastor opens the Bible in the meeting. A carefully arranged series of topics would secure more preparation on the part of the pastors, and it would also stimulate the people to the study of the Word.

"4. Where is this thing to end? Pretty soon a committee will be laying out topics for the pulpit; and we will have our ministers asked to preach through a yearly programme of texts.

"Well, if the worst must come, why not? There would be fewer old sermons preached. Pastors would be relieved of the worry and waste of time caused by the weekly hunt for a 'subject for next Sunday.' They would, many of them, preach over a far wider range of topics than they do now, and they would have a good excuse for some plain sermons on delicate subjects, which, if they were not in regular course, might be considered very personal.

"I have an experience of two years' use of a published list of topics for the prayer-meeting. It has worked well, and has done us great good. See here:

"1. The pastor studies for the prayer-meeting a great deal harder than he used to. He must. For the people are studying too, and he must bring the water from fresh springs. The stagnant pool will not do.

"2. The people study the Word more. They find topics that appeal to their present wants, and that are illustrated by their experience of the day in the shop, store, field and house. The Word has a more practical relation to every day life than before.

"3. The prayer-meetings are interesting. This results from the facts above named. Pastor and people come to it already interested. They don't have to spend three-fourths of the hour 'getting up' an interest.

"4. There is unity of thought and effort. Prayers have a point and directness caught from the subject. There is less scattering shot than under the old plan.

"5. The printed list placed in the Bibles of the people serve to keep the fact of the prayer-meeting before them. It is an announcement every time they see it. And the neat card furnishes the handiest possible invitation to strangers to come.

"Try it, brethren, and let us have the strength and interest that are born of united effort."

Dear Sir — My opinion on uniformity, etc., is shown by the fact that I, years ago, started the matter, so far as I know, without a precedent to follow, and introduced a uniform scheme in all the Presbyterian churches of Detroit, and afterward in the Presbytery started a similar scheme. I send a copy of both in another enclosure.

Could the religious papers treat the topic as the S. S. topic is now— only prayer-meeting-wise — what an incalculable help to the feeble churches, many of whom have no minister. And what an advantage in giving prominence to the spiritual and practical character of the church-meeting! But the whole thing must be flexible, not rigid or frigid; in revivals or unusual state of things must of course give way, and so to monthly concert. What a blessing if *one night* could be uniform, and the first meeting of the month be a concert for missions! ARTHUR T. PIERSON, D. D.

Detroit, Mich.

VINCENNES, IND., April 24th, 1879.

REV. L. O. THOMPSON:

Dear Sir and Brother — In my ministerial experience I have found the prayer-meeting the one most difficult to conduct satisfactorily, and yet my conviction of the very great importance of it as a meeting has been constantly increasing. I have been as conscientious in my preparation for it, and have expended as much thought and care upon it, ordinarily, as upon any other one service. I am firmly convinced that work done here is profitable, and yields large returns.

I have been much interested in and helped by your recent book on "The Prayer-Meeting," and I, for one would be heartily glad if our churches could adopt some plan by which we might have uniformity in these services, instead of the too often and largely unsatisfactory methods which have been obtained. Invited by your note to express my views, I do so in favor of the system in which you, for one, have already done most commendable work. I believe that by a uniformity of topics in our various churches, the bond of union between us would be strengthened and spiritualized, for we would feel emphasized the great fact that we are ONE in praying over God's Word, and pleading with Him on the mercy seat.

For three years I have used a printed list of topics in my prayer-meetings. My success in inducing the members to take part has not been what I have hoped for, but we are all assured that it is good to have our printed list. This is in the hands of all our members, and I frequently announce the subject on Sabbath morning, in addition. Very generally the passage is read, and thought upon, and prayed over, by those who attend the prayer-meeting. There is an advantage in having the subject known beforehand, not only by those who pray in public, and speak, but by those whose voices are not heard, but who are mighty in prayer.

Very generally the subjects have been appropriate for weeks and months at a time. If for any peculiar occasion a change is desirable, the change is easily made and announced. I shall continue to use a printed list of subjects, so long as I feel that God blesses the plan as He has done. We have a perpetual revival in our church. The prayer-meeting is loved by the people. Our attendance is over a hundred, unless something extraordinary interferes with it. I thank you most heartily for the good I have already received from your work, and pray that the abundant blessing of God may still rest on your labors.

Yours for the Master,
E. P. WHALLON.

My dear Sir — Your note of the 10th inst. is before me. I have no confident opinion to express on the question of uniform topics. The analogy between the Sunday-school and the prayer-meeting is not so close as to make it certain that what is good for one is equally good for the other. The adoption of the uniform lessons for the Sunday-school has given a new impulse and cast to the Sunday-school work, and especially to the study of all parts of the Holy Scriptures in connection therewith. I do not, however, feel sure that it will be best to keep it up always.

The uniform topics for the prayer-meeting, I should think, (without having had any experience under their adoption), might work favorably to correct the loose, helter-skelter, aimless exercises, which often fill up the hour to little good purpose. On the other hand, freedom and spontaneity are essential qualities for a profitable meeting, and there is reason to fear that, if the exercises are brought under a rule of uniformity in respect to topics, it will tend to formality and stiffness, too much like praying by the book. The golden mean is between these extremes. It seems to me well to give the churches a chance to try the experiment of coming into uniformity and concert of action, though it may be but a temporary thing. I welcome any measure which will tend to extend and intensify interest in the prayer-meetings of the church, and to deepen the spiritual tone of such exercises.

Very truly yours,

A. L. CHAPIN.

Dr. Chapin, who is president of Beloit College, and one of the editors of Johnson's "New and Universal Cyclopedia," has served on the committee that selected the subjects for the Sunday-school. It is to be hoped that the danger he thinks connected with this use may be avoided. There is no inevitable connection between "formality and stiffness" and an announced topic. "Where the Spirit of the Lord is, there is liberty."

"I can not see," writes the Rev. R. W. Fletcher, of Parma, Mich., "why uniformity in topics for the prayer-meeting would not secure all the advantages that are secured for the Sunday-school in uniformity of teaching. Beside securing these advantages, it would facilitate Christian union, and especially if we could arrange for gatherings similar to our Normal classes. It is good to study the Word together. It must certainly be good for us to unite our prayers — for all Christians of the various churches to pray together. Where we have tried it to any considerable extent in this section of the country, we have found it to be a success."

Dear Bro.— I find from experience, uniformity of topics for prayer-meeting to be an advantage in breaking up set forms of prayer, in encouraging special preparation on the part of all who take a part, especially the leader, in causing short, pointed remarks and prayers, in causing Scripture verses to be committed to memory, and repeated on the topic for the meeting, and in awakening and sustaining a lively interest generally. Respectfully,

M. V. B. VANTISDALE.
Pastor Green Valley, Ill.

CHAPTER XII.

TYPICAL PRAYER-MEETINGS.

I DESIGN here to give a variety of incidents to illustrate in one way and another the heading of this chapter, that each one may see for himself how prayer-meetings are killed, what need there is of improvement, and in what way they may be improved.

Dr. Gray, editor of the *Interior*, on his way home from the last General Assembly at Saratoga Springs, had to wait for change of cars at Schenectady, and among other things which appeared in his paper for June 5th, was a brief account of a typical prayer-meeting which he attended whilst the slow hours were creeping along :

"Thence we strayed," he wrote, "up the ancient streets of Schenectady, in search of the Reformed (Dutch) church, where a prayer-meeting was in progress. The building is modern and very graceful in architecture. Worship had begun when we entered. There were present eight men and fifty-six women. An old brother rose, and in a most melancholy tone began an exhortation which seemed interminable.

So far as it had any ideas, they were warnings to the women to repent and believe — the women, because the seven men other than himself were evidently saints. On he went, and on and on, more and more dolorous. At the end of his speech he started off on a long prayer, and at the end of the prayer began a horrible caricature of singing a hymn, which he sang solo, and only stopped after he had both missed the tune, and forgotten the words. One or two other lamentable prayers were made, and that deplorable prayer-meeting was at an end. There are doubtless many other such cases. Are not the authorities of a church greatly at fault where such misguided but well-meaning brethren are not silenced, and kept silent, in the prayer-meeting?"

This was followed by another article the week after, which showed that editor Gray was more fortunate in the next prayer-meeting that he struck:

"We gave a description," said he, "of a prayer-meeting in which were one prayer-meeting killer, seven other brethren, and fifty-six ladies, and mentioned that the affair was not very enjoyable. We have discovered another of a character very different. There were about a hundred present, of whom not over two-thirds were ladies. Where the brethren are not out-numbered by the woman over two to one, there should be no complaint made of their lack of interest in spiritual things. Well, in this prayer-meeting there was not the first syllable of prayer-meeting cant or formality. The pastor took his seat and a hymn was sung. He then said that this was to be a voluntary meeting throughout, and asked from each one present a text of Scripture which was held as specially precious. Promises, precepts, doctrines concerning Christ and Christian duty were quoted by men, women and youth, with no undue haste, but with no delay. The pastor made comment on each text—sometimes using not more than three words in referring to the pith of the Scripture idea. After a time a hymn was volunteered, and then a brief prayer which followed in the line of thought suggested by the text. Then came more Scripture sentences. It was observable that the text followed leading thoughts, one text suggesting another. The meeting was closed by a few appropriate remarks by the pastor and a hymn volunteered by one of the company. The most alert interest prevailed from first to last. There was not a moment wasted, nor one in which the pleasing and varied movement of thought, prayer and singing, flagged or dragged. It would require a minister of extraordinary powers in the pulpit to hold attention so closely, and afford at once so much profit and pleasure."

By this time his paper had got to Schenectady, and as is supposable, called forth a spirited rejoinder. Dr. Gray, however, as he always does, rose equal to the occasion, and kindly planted a few blows upon the layman's letter, by way of improvement. Both are now given as they originally appeared:

"*That Prayer-meeting at Schenectady.*

" In glancing over your issue of the 5th, my eye rested upon a paragraph in which you pay your respects, somewhat severely, it strikes me, to this ancient and time-honored burgh, and also to a prayer-meeting into which you found your way. Without stopping to criticise your remarks upon our city, calculated as they are, to give a stranger not only an unfavorable but a decidedly erroneous view of its general appearance, permit me a word or two upon your remarks upon the prayer-meeting referred to. In the first place, we do not question the correctness of the statement concerning the number present, which is placed definitely at sixty-four, namely eight men and fifty-six woman. In no other way could this result have been reached but by careful, conscientious counting. To have enhanced the interest connected with this important statement, the number of children present (if any), of each sex, should also have been mentioned, as the question will possibly for years to come, plague the minds of the readers of *The Interior:* Do or do not children, as a rule, form a part of the audience of a Schenectady prayer-meeting? particularly in the Reformed (Dutch) denomination. Such an omission is unfortunate. On one point, however, you are more precise. You state that 'an old brother addressed the meeting.' This is true, and if your writer were as intimately acquainted with him as one of those whom he addressed, his strictures, we are very sure, would have been tinctured with more of that charity so highly commended by St. Paul. The 'brother' alluded to, has passed his fourscore and four, and although the weight of so great an age begins to press heavily upon him, his heart still beats strong and warm for the cause of his Master, whom he has so long served; and for his much-loved church. Residing as he does at a distance from the city, it is but seldom that he attends an evening meeting, perhaps three or four times in a twelve-month. Is it strange, then, that when he is able to come, he feels an earnest desire to perform what he feels to be a sacred duty. The evidences of his failing mind only serve to win to him still more closely, those who have learned to love and venerate the aged disciple. His voice, in song or exhortation we know will be heard in its accustomed place not many times in the future, for it will soon be hushed in death. Because he 'misses the tune,' or 'forgets the words,' of one of the hymns he learned in his younger days, shall he be silenced, as your writer unfeelingly suggests? Because he tells the same old story two or three times a year, shall the privilege to do so, which he so highly prizes, be denied him? What sort of an estimate would any of us be likely to put upon the Christianity of the early church if the venerable apostle John, after his oft-repeated injunction, 'Little children, love one another,' had received from the elders the reproof, 'Misguided brother, your remarks are not edifying. You had better refrain from speaking in meeting.' Our brother's evident sincerity and trembling voice made, it seems, no appeal to the sympathy of a fellow disciple. But may we ask why, in a gathering of 'two or three' met in the name of the Head of the church, did not our brother from Chicago feel it a privilege to bear his 'testimony.' If the meeting was cold, perhaps a word, or prayer, uttered by him, might have fanned the smouldering embers into an ardent flame.

"LAYMAN."

"REMARKS.

"Such an aged saint as our correspondent describes has a right to tolerance, to almost any extent, of the infirmities which come with great age. The writer did not suspect an age so great, and being a stranger, casually happening into the meeting, could only sketch it in the light that there appeared. It was furthest from his purpose to attack any one. The prayer-meeting was but a typical one, though perhaps extreme, of a class; and it was employed merely as an illustration. The fact remains, however, that our good contributor is displeased that we should refer in terms not commendatory to a prayer-meeting in which only one-seventh of those present were men, and in which the services were gloomy and depressing, and not by any means only because a good old man indulged in a talk which was not interesting. Such prayer-meetings need stirring up. If they will not bear a photographic description in a newspaper, how will they bear the continual review of the Master?"

I followed these pieces with a letter to Dr. Gray which was published on July 3d, under the caption

"*Other Schenectadys.*"

"I carefully laid aside that article on the Schenectady prayer-meeting which lately appeared in *The Interior*. I knew that it was foreordained to become famous. A second article, the week following, to describe a meeting in which ' there was not the first syllable of prayer-meeting cant or formality' only confirmed me in that opinion. That article was also marked and laid aside. To-day comes *The Interior*, with article number three, entitled. 'That prayer-meeting at Schenectady.' 'I told you so.' That, too, is marked and laid aside. And now that the ball is fairly got in motion I suppose other contributions in the same line are in order. Here is mine: I was narrating the spicy contents of articles one and two to a retired minister of our city, as introductory to the reading of number three. 'Well,' said he, 'that reminds me of a prayer-meeting I went to conduct, by invitation, in this city not long ago. When I got to the meeting I found but one man present; all the rest were women. I did not know him, but, seeing him there, I took him to be a Christian, and called on him to pray. He responded. Presently another man came in, and thinking that if he was not a Christian he would not be there, I likewise called on him. He too offered prayer.' Now, the full force of his three-men prayer-meeting story is only brought out in connection with the fact that the good brother who undertook to lead the meeting had suffered a partial stroke of paralysis while on a visit to Missouri over a year ago, and it so happened on this particular night that his tongue somewhat failed him and refused to articulate distinctly. And now, that I am speaking about him, I may say to the great praise and honor of this retired minister, who has preached the Gospel over half a century, that though he is nearly an octogenarian, yet he is as regular and prompt in his attendance on Sabbath and prayer-meeting services as the clock. If he is not present, I know in advance he is sick, or conducting a meeting for somebody else. What a continuous sermon his example is preaching!"

There is a type of another meeting not far outside of the State of New York. A young girl, visiting a church after an absence of five years, wrote back to her father, who had been its pastor, that she found the prayer-meeting just where it was when they left. Its members sat in just the same seats, in the same parts of the house, the same hymns were sung, the same brethren repeated their well-conned prayers of the days past, and the story-telling brethren had just the same reminiscences and experiences to relate that she had become familiar with half a decade of years ago. Now it is self-evident that nothing else in the world than duty (what a grand thing to see a life shaped and controlled by duty) keeps up the attendance of meetings like these, as juiceless as a dried-up orange. But is there not a better way?

In closing this chapter, and as introductory to the

one that shall follow, I will give an account of a minister's visit to a neighboring prayer-meeting, which was published in *The Preacher and Homiletic Monthly*, Jan., 1879, and this account will show that the prayer-meeting service is as difficult of management as any connected with the church.

To the editor, Rev. J. K. Funk — I enjoyed the luxury of attending a prayer-meeting a few evenings since, outside of my own church. It is a celebrated one, known throughout our city for its size and vigor. Many hundred conversions are reported as having taken place in it during the past few years. As on this evening I held no meeting, I thought I would go down and study the secret of my neighbor's success in the management of his prayer services. I was twice surprised during my hour's stay.

First, I saw nearly half the large audience slip out of the room during the first quarter hour of the exercise, and this because the pastor was not present. In vain the leader, who proved a good man for the place, reminded the audience that "One, greater than our pastor has promised to meet with us." Either, thought I, that retiring audience did not believe the promise, or did not come to meet that greater One. In either case, there seemed to me to be a fatal mistake in the teachings those people had been accustomed to hear. No congregation who gather in the regular place for prayer once a week, rightly instructed, will desert the meeting because the leader they expected is not present. A crowd is not sure proof of success. Even conversions are but people starting right; if the work ends with starting, it is a miserable failure.

Secondly, I was again surprised at an onslaught one of the speakers made on my favorite revival hymn,

" Come, humble sinner, in whose breast," etc.

Said he, " That hymn sends a shiver all through me whenever I hear it read or sung, for it expresses a doubt of a repentant sinner's acceptance with God. The sinner in the hymn is represented as approaching God distrustingly. He lacks faith, the very essential of acceptance. Then, in the last stanza, he is made to express joy at the thought of meeting destruction while seeking divine mercy:

" That were to die (delightful thought) !
As sinners never die."

As if that would be any satisfaction to a ruined soul ! Really that hymn, after that speech, did not seem so faultless to me as it did before. But is the prayer-meeting a place for criticism, even though it be of the above nature ? A CLERGYMAN.

CHAPTER XIII.

THE PRAYER-MEETING A GROWTH.

IT is not to be looked for that our prayer-meetings shall become all of a sudden just what they ought to be in spiritual profit and attractive power. The model prayer-meeting is a plant of slow growth. It is not a century plant, neither is it an annual; but it takes years to bring it to maturity and full fruitfulness.

The pastor and the people need to entertain similar ideas about the prayer-meeting, and its true place in the church, that thus they may co-operate, and zealously work together for their attainment. For instance, if the people think that the prayer-meeting ought to be an "evangelistic service," and the pastor thinks that it ought mainly to be a meeting for spiritual conference and edification, or *vice versa;* then it is hardly to be looked for that they shall develop much harmony and enthusiasm in seeking their ideals. But if pastor and people can unite on the same ideals, it may reasonably be expected that they will do all within their power to realize them.

There is, too, in every church, a greater amount of

receptive gifts than of donative. There are more habitual listeners, than habitual participants. There is a rich capacity for song, and speech, and prayer, that lies dormant in the church. It will take time to develop this wealth of resources in the church, and bring it into efficient service. Dr. James B. Shaw, pastor of the Brick Church, Rochester, has given this excellent advice to the members of his church, "Consent to be habitually silent, only after making the most strenuous and repeated endeavors to acquire self-possession. You may be a very useful Christian, and yet be unheard here, but if you *can* overcome your infirmity, it will greatly increase your usefulness." The Rev. J. K. Funk, editor of *The Preacher and Homiletic Monthly*, reports Mr. Beecher as saying, "The good prayer-meeting is the result of years of patient work. Our prayer-meeting in Plymouth Church for the first five years of my labor amounted to little; at the end of the next five years it did not amount to much. But then my work began to tell. I had to train up men in my idea of a prayer-meeting."

Christian experience is the work of the Holy Spirit in us, to which testimony should be given in the prayer-meeting, for the profit and instruction of the household of faith. Now, it is evident the bringing into efficient service this talent, will of necessity add to the interest, the instruction, the spiritual refreshment, and the attractive power of the prayer-meeting.

But it is needful, also, to instruct the people in the elements of a good prayer-meeting. Some are apt to speak too long, or to pray at too great length, and thus to repeat themselves and become prosy, as well as deprive others of the privilege of taking part. In the interview referred to above, Mr. Beecher said, "The prayer-meeting is for the edification of a great many more than those who pray. I know just what kind of a prayer-meeting I want. When one talks or prays too long, I manage, usually without giving offence, to drop an effective hint. I sometimes say, as the long-winded brother is taking his seat, that was a good prayer — *the first five minutes*. If one is speaking too long, and has got into a rut and can't get out, which often happens in a prayer-meeting, I put a question to him to divert his thoughts, and am answering my own question before he is aware of it. Then I have got the reins again. There must be no dullness. Better have dullness in the regular Sunday service than in the prayer-meeting. I prepare specially for these meetings. I usually talk without getting up off my chair, in an off-handed manner, on some questions which involve religious experience. I seek to answer questions — encourage the asking of questions which have to do with personal experience. In this way the meetings are instructive and inspiring."

CHAPTER XIV.

How Shall we get Members to take Part?

PERHAPS too high an estimate is placed upon speaking gifts. The gift of eloquence is a remarkable power which ambitious men earnestly covet, and but few possess. A speaker at the bar, on the rostrum, in the political arena, or upon the floors of legislative chambers, may speak for applause, and receive it, and be stimulated by it to higher efforts; but such influences and actions find no place in the room for public prayer and social praise. Are Christians, then, to make no efforts to speak, but contentedly remain silent? No. Their speaking should not be a mere duty, but a pleasure and privilege, rendered such by a fulness of love and heart, out of whose abundance prayer, praise, and testimony shall spring on winged words. Why should not the motives which prompt men to praise God, and to speak and pray when the church is gathered together in the name of Christ, be still higher than the ambition for power and applause? It is, and would be so esteemed, if our lives were more holy, and our efforts were more judiciously and regularly put forth.

Inasmuch, then, as those motives are absent which stimulate men to seek possession of the speaking gifts in other departments of life, how shall we get men to take part, when in more than a majority of cases, speaking is to them a heavy duty, and no pleasure? The attendance may be good, fully one-half of the whole membership, or even more, and yet the number of those accustomed to speak and pray may be distressingly small.

Now it may be that there are cases where some professors live such lives — in a backslidden state — as to totally unfit them for taking any part in exercises of a holy nature, unless they act the part of hypocrites. The lips of some, it may be, are closed by the variance between their accepted creeds and daily life. Such need to be revived, to have the evil spirit cast out, and their tongues to be touched with a live coal from off the altar, and then their lips will be opened to praise God, and thank Him for His marvellous mercy. But I would be far from saying that this is true of all the silent ones in our prayer-meetings. By no means. Some very excellent and useful Christians, from peculiarities of temperament, have never attempted to speak; or having attempted it, are utterly discouraged; and yet to the praise of such, be it said, they are still regular attendants upon the prayer-meeting.

But how can we assist those who ought to take part, and have no sufficient reasons for permanent silence, so that they shall become serviceable in this department of Christian life? A few suggestions only are here offered in this direction.

When members are first converted, that is the golden moment in which to urge them to speak of Christ and for Christ, and to bless God out of such fulness of heart as His own Spirit has produced. And it will be wise, I think, for the leader, after such testimony on their part, to see them and counsel with them in a private and friendly way, so that if they are at all discouraged, and determined ever after to keep silent, the nature of their difficulties may be examined into, and their imaginary obstacles removed. Some of these hindrances have been presented in the previous volume, as well as some hints suggested in a chapter on "Helps to Speaking in Public." You should counsel those who have taken part for the first time, not to be discouraged by grammatical mistakes, nor repeat to correct them. Bishop Simpson's rule is excellent; not to stop for correction unless something false or utterly vicious has been said. But if something of the latter kind has been spoken, of course it ought to be corrected. Thus, I think, that a minister whom I heard in prayer, by a slip of the tongue, say — if at all conscious of it — that he praised God because He had turned us "from darkness to light, and from the power of God unto Satan," ought not to have permitted the last clause to remain uncorrected; but all mistakes of a grammatical or figurative nature may be safely allowed to pass until greater freedom and fluency shall give a better and clearer use of language. And there is such a thing as being over fastidious. Grammatical proprieties and rhetorical elegancies are poor offsets for zeal and whole heartedness. "We ought," says Spurgeon, " to leave room for enthusiasts, even if they violate every rule of grammar. A grand blundering, hammering, thundering, whole-hearted Boanerges, is worth a dozen prim, reverend gentlemen, meek as milk and water, and soft as boiled parsnips."

But a very useful answer to the subject of our chapter, I have found to consist in arranging for a meeting in which a large number of those who have not taken part previously, are urged to speak, and be sure not to use more than two or three minutes. Tell them if they go beyond three minutes, you will be obliged to stop them, and this for the evident reason that they must not trespass on the time that belongs to others. And again, at the beginning of the meeting, announce it as a rule that no one is expected or will be permitted to consume more than three minutes; and let those who have been previously urged to speak understand that they have perfect liberty to stop before their three minutes are up. Remarks two minutes long shall have the preference to four minutes. The shorter the better. A man is wonderfully helped, when he feels in advance that if his thoughts and his words fail him, he need not beat about the bush in that terrible ordeal of an attempt at a long address; but may stop at once, and shield by silence what would otherwise be a grieved and a wounded heart. It will be helpful to them, also, if each one has a text of Scripture — not all using the same text — on which to found his brief remarks.

The following plan is given in illustration of this method, and is simply the account of an actual meeting. The subject is, "Result of Abiding in Christ," as contained in the passage found in St. John's Gospel fifteenth chapter, from the fifth to the sixteenth verses, inclusive. The hymns are selected from "Gospel Hymns and Sacred Songs," and are designed to be in harmony, so far as that is possible, with the subjects which they follow. If each part in this plan takes about three minutes, the length of the meeting will be an hour, and if less time is consumed in the singing, it can be filled with more prayer, so that in no case need the assembly be kept beyond the hour :

1. OPENING HYMN — No. 25.
    "We praise Thee, O God! for the Son of Thy Love,
    For Jesus who died, and is now gone above."
2. SCRIPTURE LESSON — Psalm 146th, and prayer by the pastor or leader of the meeting.
3. HYMN — No. 48, verses 1, 2.
    "Saviour, more than life to me,
    I am clinging, clinging close to Thee."
4. FIRST RESULT OF ABIDING IN CHRIST — Fruitfulness, John 15 : 5, 6 and 8. (Remarks not to exceed three minutes.)
5. HYMN — No. 104.
    "So let our lips and lives express,
    The Holy Gospel we profess."
6. SECOND RESULT — Prayer is answered. John 15 : 7.
7. HYMN — No. 93.
    "More holiness give me,
    More strivings within."
8. PRAYER.
9. THIRD RESULT — Love. John 15: 9, 12.
10. HYMN — No. 46, verses 1, 2 and 4.
    "Oh sing of His mighty love."
11. FOURTH RESULT — Obedience. John 15 : 10.
12. HYMN — No. 26. "Something for Jesus." Verses 3 and 4.
    "Give me a faithful heart — likeness to Thee —
    That each departing day henceforth may see."
13. PRAYER.
14. FIFTH RESULT — Joy. John 15 : 11, 12 and 13.

15. Hymn — No. 100.
>"My heart that was heavy and sad,
>Was made to rejoice and be glad."

16. Sixth Result — Fellowship. John 15: 14, 15.

17. Hymn — No. 114; verses 1, 2 and 3.
>"Blest be the tie that binds
>Our hearts in Christian love;
>The fellowship of kindred minds
>Is like to that above."

18. Seventh Result — Service. John 15: 16.

19. Hymn — No. 122.
>"Work, for the night is coming;
>Work through the morning hours;
>Work while the dew is sparkling;
>Work, 'mid springing flowers;
>Work when the day grows brighter,
>Work in the glowing sun;
>Work, for the night is coming,
>When man's work is done."

20. Prayer.

21. Doxology —
>"Praise God from whom all blessings flow;
>Praise him, all creatures here below;
>Praise him above, ye heavenly host;
>Praise Father, Son and Holy Ghost."

Benediction.

CHAPTER XV.

MONTHLY CONCERT FOR MISSIONS.

THE work of evangelizing the world is so important, its duty so pressing, and its influence so various, that the monthly meeting for missions should be made as attractive and interesting as possible. It was the command of the risen Saviour to His disciples that they should preach the Gospel in Jerusalem, in all Judea, in Samaria, and to the uttermost parts of the earth. And for this particular work they were to receive power after that the Holy Ghost had come upon them. In obedience to the command of the Master to wait for the promise of the Father, they continued with one accord in prayer and supplication until the day of Pentecost was fully come, "when they were all filled with the Holy Ghost and began to speak with other tongues, as the Spirit gave them utterance."

And for the successful conduct of this work the church of to-day equally needs the gift of tongues and the baptism of the Spirit; the gift of tongues as acquired by the missionaries through years of study to qualify them to speak in the various languages wherewith the children of men express their thoughts, and the baptism of the Spirit, in order to make the telling of the "old, old story of Jesus and His love," a savor of life unto life to all that hear. "The church has received her marching orders," as the Duke of Wellington said, "and cannot help herself." The meeting of the church, on stated occasions, to consider the cause of missions, its encouragements and hindrances, and to pray for success in its promotion, is a duty which lies in the line of this command, and is so essential in its nature that her own life and spiritual prosperity at home are intimately connected with it.

The monthly meeting of the church for prayer, in behalf of missions will have an important influence upon the work at home. It will enlarge the mind, and enrich the heart. To go outside of the narrow limits of our own church walls, and to take in the spiritual wants of the surrounding community, is well and wise ; and then to pass from there to the wants of several cities until we include a state, and from a single state to include the wants of all the states in a great Union is wise and well, but finally to pass beyond the boundaries of our own beloved land, and then to take in the wants of all lands, until the globe has been encircled is wisest and best, and as demonstrated by the history of the church is most fruitful in spiritual results. But our duty does not go beyond this world. It does not extend to Venus or to Mars — to inferior or superior planets — but it does include the world. And the Christian Church, loyal to Christ, should be eager and anxious to take the whole world into the arms of her faith, prayer and endeavor, and lift it up to God.

The influence of the concert for prayer, is equally marked upon mission fields. Missionaries encounter many and peculiar difficulties in the prosecution of their work. Prayer and sympathy help them in various ways. It may be worth our while to see how the missionaries themselves regard this matter; for they are qualified to speak of its influence upon them and their work. The Rev. B. Labaree gives the following as reasons, "Why we ask you to pray for Persia":

"1. Because of special encouragements in the past history of this mission. Many remarkable revivals, hundreds of souls in whom the new life in Christ has been begun; numerous evangelical churches as beacon fires of the Gospel in Oroomiah, Tabreez, Hamadan; some hopeful converts and multitudes of inquirers among Mussulmans — all these are the fruits of the church's prayer for Persia.

"2. Because of special discouragements and obstacles; such as (1) the bigotry of the masses and the misrule and oppression of the governing classes; (2) the danger of persecution and even death to Mussulman converts; (3) the deceitfulness and hypocrisy of the Persian character, greatly embarrassing us in our labors for Mussulmans; (4) the activity and influence of the Papists and other foes.

"3. Because the influence of Christian Governments in Persia, is less than in Mohammaden lands. We are the more shut up to direct dependence on Divine Power.

"4. Because we see how prayer inclined a king of ancient Persia to promote the building of Jerusalem's walls. May not that same might move the present rulers to aid in building our modern Zion? We especially want their non-interference in erecting our new seminary.

"Pray, too for the missionaries and native preachers, that we may all be full of faith and the Holy Ghost."

Let the unbelieving say what they will about answer to prayer, the church knows the value of prayer by a precious experience.

"A few examples will be given," says the Rev. Hollis Read, formerly a missionary of the American Board, "where prayer seems to have been answered on a remote part of the globe, on the very day, and perhaps the same hour, it was offered.

"On the first Monday of January, 1833, there was an extraordinary and unaccountable religious movement on the minds of a class of natives who had been for a few months under Christian instruction at Ahmednuggur. The writer, then the only missionary at the station, invited all who wished to be Christians, to meet him for religious conversation and inquiry, when, to his surprise, thirteen responded to the call, all, apparently, deeply convicted of sin, and wishing to be pointed to the Saviour. The number was in a few days increased to sixteen, most of whom subsequently became members of the church.

"'I was called up at midnight, on the first Monday of January,' says the Rev. Mr. Spaulding of Ceylon, 'by one of the girls of the Oodooville school, and informed that the whole school was assembled in the large lecture-room, for prayer. On going thither, and seeing all present to hear what the Lord would command them, I found them in a most interesting state of mind; and this was the beginning of the great revival of religion in Ceylon. Inquiring how this thing originated, I found the larger girls (the younger ones having retired), had assembled for their evening prayer-meeting, and not being able to separate at the usual hour, the interest became so intense that one after another called up a friend to share in the good feeling, till, at length, the whole school were assembled.'

"The first Monday of January, 1838, presented a scene of thrilling interest at the Sandwich Islands. At the rising of the sun, the church and congregation at Honolulu, filling one of the largest houses of worship on the islands, united in solemn prayer for the outpouring of the Spirit of God. And thence followed a series of protracted meetings throughout the islands, and a general revival of religion blessed the entire nation. This was the beginning of what is known as 'the great revival.' By midsummer, more than five thousand had been received into the church, and two thousand four hundred stood propounded for membership. Though there had been some favorable indications of a spiritual movement some time previous, and the preceding Sabbath, had been a day of unusual interest at Honolulu, yet we may date the beginning of the great revival on that day. Now the windows of heaven were opened and the refreshing rain came! and as the fruits of the remarkable work there were gathered with the churches, (1838–40) twenty thousand persons; and more than three thousand remained as candidates for admission.

"On the first Monday of January, 1846, two of the

older girls in Miss Fisk's school at Ooroomiah, linger after morning prayers. She inquires the reason; finds they feel themselves to be lost sinners, and ask that they may spend the day in retirement. In a few days they are rejoicing in the hope of sins forgiven. Five others come to Miss Fisk the same day and ask what they shall do to be saved; and, with no knowledge of what had taken place in the school, a considerable number of Mr. Stoddard's scholars came to him with the same inquiry. From this hour we date the commencement of the present powerful and extensive revival of religion, which has already prevailed, not only in the two seminaries, but the city of Ooroomiah and the adjacent villages, and has spread even among the mountains, and already numbers more than a hundred and fifty converts; to say nothing of the deep and far-reaching moral influence which this religious movement has produced on the Nestorian mind in general, and the conviction of the power of evangelical truth. Nor was this all; just two years before (Monday, January, 1844,), there were decisive indications of the mighty workings of the Spirit at the same station, producing a happy effect on the hearts of the native Christians and missionaries, but resulting in the conversion of only one individual, and he a young man the most unlikely to be thus affected. But he afterwards became a most efficient helper in the mission, and, perhaps, did more than any other one, to prepare the way for the great work now in progress. God first prepares his instruments, then does his work.

"On the same day, (1846), the Spirit was poured out from on high, upon the Choctaw Indians. A pleasant state of things existed a few days previous. but on Monday (Jan. 5th), the Spirit came down in power, and a mighty work began, and did not end till more than two hundred were gathered into the church, which did not number before over seven hundred. 'Before they call, I will answer, and while they are yet speaking, I will hear.'"

How, then, shall we make the Monthly Concerts for missions so interesting and attractive that the people shall always come to them with a feeling of delight, and be unwilling to have them unrepresented in the scheme of annual topics? I will give some answers that have proved very helpful in my own church, and which upon correspondence I have found to be equally helpful in the experience of other pastors:

1. Solicit annually some person, or persons, to represent the respective mission fields for whose support

your church is enlisted, and let these keep their fields in mind during the year and solicit and treasure up such facts and items as shall make the particular consideration of their field by the church full of instruction and pleasureable profit.

2. Get some one that is skilled at drawing, to make a large map in outline of each field, and hang it up where all may see it, and then having done so use it by giving a graphic description of the country, its climate, surroundings, characteristics, etc.

3. Appoint some one each month to prepare a paper on the field to be considered. (See "Prayer-Meeting And Its Improvement," page 205, *seq.*)

4. Let the leader, and as many as he can enlist in the arrangement, come to the meeting full of knowledge on the field, and a vivid conception of facts; and then there will be no lack of speakers, nor of interest in the meetings.

5. Draw your facts from every available source, commit them to memory, heat them like iron and then speak from the abundance of your resources. Never read any printed stuff to the people; for nothing will sooner kill the interest in the Monthly Concert than such a habit. It is a sure sign that you have lost your own interest, and besides are getting too lazy to make preparation for the meeting, and a sustained interest

in it. * A pastor writes me, whose Monthly Concert is of unusual profit and interest, "I always go ready to talk an hour on missions, if it is necessary."

6. Have some one especially appointed to make an address or talk upon the particular field, and its various mission stations, the personnel of its missionary force, past results and the present outlook. Occasionally vary this plan so as to have, in the place of one address, half a dozen three minute talks from as many different persons, each one of whom has got hold of some facts, and like Elihu is full of matter; the Spirit within him constraining him.

7. But in case all these should fail you, be ready yourself to fill up the time with such information, so heated by meditation, that you cannot help but speak with enthusiasm; for such a habit will always rescue a meeting from occasional failures and make it, year in and year out, equally profitable and attractive. There will then be no danger that the interest in missions will die out in your church.

---

* I am not at liberty to mention his name, because he does not wish his people to know the fulness of his own preparation for *every* meeting, lest it should keep them from equal thoroughness in preparation. But the point I wish to make is this: If both pastor and people come to the meeting with such fulness of preparation and such abundance of resources, it cannot be otherwise than that the Monthly Concert will hold its place among the most interesting of all the weekly meetings.

8. Finally, take up a penny collection for the cause of missions. If each person present give but a penny — remember the widow's mite — the aggregate during the year will be considerable, and consecrated by your prayers and the prayers of your people, who shall estimate the fruit thereof? At this stage of the meeting, after the people have been fully informed of the respective needs of the mission fields, it seems to me, they are prepared to give intelligently, and take a pleasure in giving, to the pecuniary support of the great work, whose object, in obedience to the risen Saviour's commands, is the evangelization of the whole earth. Nor need any one fear that this will diminish aught from the stated contributions of the church towards missions; it will enlarge it the rather. "Many mickles make a muckle."

And in order to give a tabular view of the results by the above method, I will insert two sketches of Monthly Concert meetings, the first on Mexico, and the second on India. The outline on Mexico is the account of a meeting held in the First Presbyterian Church, Chicago, which was kindly sent me by the pastor, Rev. Arthur Mitchell, D.D., in response to my note after the said meeting had been held:

I — MEXICO.

March 5th, 1879.

1. Hymn.
2. Prayer — By the pastor.
3. Hymn.
4. Reading — Romans 10: 1-18.
5. A Paper on Mexico — Read, (after brief preparatory and extemporaneous remarks) by R. C. Hamill, M. D. The paper was about twenty or twenty-five minutes long.
6. A Talk on Mexico — Its missions; their success, the present missionary force, etc. By the pastor; in the midst of which, a brother speaks out, as in a conversation at home, to correct or enlarge some word of the speaker, by means of a question; or the speaker in turn, puts a question to any one who may be better informed on a particular point, than himself. This occupied twenty to twenty-five minutes.
7. Two prayers in succession, by brethren, as called upon by the pastor.
8. Hymn and Benediction.

II — INDIA.

April 2d, 1879.

1. Hymn — (Gospel Hymns, No. 2.) No. 81.
   "Watchman tell me does the morning
   Of fair Zion's glory dawn?"
2. Scripture — Matt. 13: 31-33; 44-58. Prayer by the pastor.
3. Hymn — No. 21.
   "Lo! the day of God is breaking;
   See the gleaming from afar."

4. A Paper on India — Written by a lady—read by a gentleman.
5. Prayer.
6. Hymn —(Gospel Hymns and Sacred Songs.) No. 78.
   "One offer of salvation
   To all the world make known."
7. Three short talks. Time, three minutes each.
8. Prayer.
9. Three additional short talks. Time, three minutes each.
10. Hymn — (Gospel Hymns and Sacred Songs.) No. 65.
    "Brightly beams our Father's mercy.
    From His lighthouse ever more."
11. A brief statement of results, or a summing up of the chief points gained in India during the last year. By the pastor. Thus, Henry Martyn once said, "If I ever see a Hindoo converted to Jesus Christ, I shall see something more nearly approaching the resumption of a dead body than anything I have ever yet seen." To-day there are about 500,000 native Christians in India. The rate of growth has been, in 1852, 128,000; 1862, 213,000; 1872, 318,000; 1878, 500,000. The entire number of conversions in 1878, was 60,000.
12. Collection.
13. Hymn —(Gospel Hymns No. 2.) No. 8.
    "Jesus shall reign where'er the sun
    Does his successive journeys run;
    His kingdom spread from shore to shore,
    Till moons shall wax and wane no more."
14. Benediction.

CHAPTER XVI.

A Text-Meeting.

THE Bible is a book we should seek to illustrate by personal experience, as much as possible. The evangelical church is zealously engaged in four enterprises of unsurpassed importance, and these are — to preach the Gospel to every creature, to supply every individual with a copy of the Bible, to put every one in the way of reading and studying its pages, and finally to assist each one, so far as human instrumentalities can do so, to a practical understanding of its pure precepts.

The Monthly Concert will bring into review the results of work in the great missionary world of modern times, and its now rapid conquests in the heathen world; and in order to have the claims and needs of the Christian world presented, it might not be injudicious to have occasionally a meeting for the home field. The disciples were commanded to begin their work at Jerusalem. The first field always to be cultivated is the home field, and then the missionary and the heathen fields.

The work of supplying the world with Bibles has progressed to the extent, that a few years ago it was reported that one family out of every five had been supplied. Estimating an average of four persons to every family, we see that about one out of every twenty persons owns a Bible. The estimated population of the globe is about 1,137,000,000, so that about 56,850,000 have been supplied. Or, if we take the number of Bibles that the various societies have printed, we get substantially the same result. The American Bible Society has printed 33,125,760 Bibles during the last sixty years, and the British Society 46,000,000 during the last fifty years. A great work remains before the lovers of the Bible, to circulate it to such extent as to make it possible for every one to own a copy.

A certain bishop in the Catholic Church delivered a lecture a few months ago, to show that their church was a church without a Bible, and did not need it; and in a lecture delivered by him on self-education, at another time, among the books named which each one ought to own, the Bible was significantly omitted; but when the entire world save the Catholic Church shall have been supplied, it too, will be forced to abandon its rule of relying upon tradition alone, and permit its laity to own the Bible, and to use it in obedience to that command of the Saviour, "Search the Scriptures; for in them ye think ye have eternal life: and they are they which testify of me." John 5 : 39.

As encouragements to the reading of the Bible, we have various departments of labor, such as expository preaching, Sunday-school instruction, teacher's meetings, Bible institutes, normal classes, topical prayer-meetings, and conferences for "Bible Readings." But notwithstanding all, there is much neglect in the reading of the Bible. Not every one that owns a Bible, reads it. Upon the covers of many a one has the dust gathered so thickly "that anywhere you might write," as Spurgeon says, "the word damnation." Or it is so elaborately gotten up, and so heavily clasped, that weak hands can never remove it from the display table and open its plated clasps; or it may be suffered to lie in the bottom of the trunk by the traveller or the schoolboy away from home. If we could only convince people that in more senses than one there is a "hidden prize" in the Bible for them, they would more eagerly read it to discover this "pearl of great price." *The Intelligencer* gives an authentic incident, over the initials of S. G., which illustrates this in a beautiful and touching manner:

"'Here is a new Bible,' said my mother, the day I went to college. 'You are going away from home, and will have many temptations. Now, my son, just as we are separating, I have one request to make. Will you read in it every day?' As I turned to examine the elegant clasps and binding, I saw tears in mother's eyes — tears which she was vainly trying to keep back. Then I firmly resolved to read a chapter, daily.

"College introduced a set of companions entirely new to me. A livelier, merrier company never distinguished college walls. I was an extravagant lover of fun, and could always raise a laugh, so that I soon gained the reputation of a wit. We led a jolly life, amusing ourselves often in secret — to the cost of others, and unconscious sacrifice of self. If we read anything, it was always of a humorous nature. We never ventured to dwell on serious subjects, dreading a snare. Flagrant offences were, however, avoided, and like one of our friends of the present age, we could say, 'College is fine with one exception, the business of recitations!'

"But I was so well prepared, so far beyond most of my classmates, that I managed to sustain myself without study and without public disgrace.

"Mother's letters were very affectionate, and she wrote often, but I always looked anxiously ahead, so as to 'skip' any part suspected of solemnity and advice. In the course I was pursuing, I could not possibly bear it.

"In vacation I returned home. After the usual greetings of welcome, my trunk and wardrobe passed through mother's ordeal. Her careful hand unfolded each article. I stood by and felt proud at her praises of my neatness and order.

"At the bottom of the trunk, under everything else, she found the Bible, and cheerfully inquired if I had remembered her request. I was speechless; she unclasped it and opened it to the middle. I started in surprise, for there were hidden two beautiful five dollar notes, one crossing the other. I never shall forget the expession of her face as she softly said, 'I wanted to give my son a pleasant surprise when away from home.'

"Mother died suddenly. I cannot doubt that she has been in heaven for many years; but I thank God that I was first able to ask her forgiveness and show true repentance, and that she lived to see me a preacher of the Bible, delighting most of all to tell what peace the Gospel can give to sinners.

"I remember once looking up from a sermon I was writing, and finding her eyes fixed on me from the next room. She said with a smile, 'I have lived to see my son a minister of Christ, and it is happiness enough for earth.'

"I was my mother's only child, and she was a widow."

And finally, the church desires to stimulate Bible reading with a view to its practical understanding. Before the days of printing, many texts and letters were illuminated, traced as they had been upon the parchments in silver, gold, and brilliant colorings. So, likewise, the Christian may illuminate his Bible; those texts which have a peculiar individual experience connected with them, should be marked, and treasured in memory. Hunters, we are told, blaze their way through a forest that they may make a familiar road. We may well believe that the thrice repeated question, "Simon, son of Jonas, lovest thou me more than these?" never departed from the memory of Peter, but always served to recall his experience connected with denial of the Lord, and those days that intervened from the time that he went out and wept bitterly, until the day he again met his risen Lord, and was so graciously assured of his restoration. May we not suppose that the Ethiopian eunuch ever cherished the most lively remembrance of Isaiah 53d, as Philip had explained it unto him? Must we not believe that ever after, when he turned to that Scripture, mental pictures of the road to

Gaza, the chariot, the deacon, the sermon that led him to Christ, his own confession and baptism, passed before his mind in vivid array? And in our own experience, if there is a particular passage that has brought us to Jesus, how appropriate to mark and prize it. If there are texts that have comforted us in the day of sorrow and distress, or in the day of trial and tribulation — falling like dew upon the thirsty soul — shall we ever forget these, and not note them with a mark more enduring than Cretan? Do you not think that the Ironside soldier in Cromwell's army, whose Bible stopped a bullet on the way to his heart, at verses nine and ten of Eccles. eleventh chapter, would ever forget that fact, and not peculiarly remember the meaning of that passage? Rom. 13 : 13, was an illuminated text in the life and experience of St. Augustine. Of all chapters, Isaiah 53d, was most valued by that wit, sinner, and penitent, the Earl of Rochester. I. Tim. 1 : 15, was the favorite text of Bilney, the martyr — and had its treasured memories. I. Tim. 1 : 17, it is said, "was the particular text which led to the conversion of the elder President Edwards." Rom. 3 : 26, was a text of precious memory, and peculiarly cherished by the poet Cowper. Eph. 3 : 20, came home with peculiar force to the historian, D'Aubigne, as accidentally read by him while stopping at an inn. The great illuminated text of Luther, and of the Protestant Reformation, was Rom. 5 : 1 ; "Therefore being justified by faith, we have peace with God through our Lord Jesus Christ." Just before Mr. Bliss left us for the last time, he handed me an album for my autograph, and there I found Is. 50: 7, to be Moody's illuminated text, written by his own hand; and that of Mr. Sankey's was Is. 35 : 10. And so there are, doubtless, particular passages in the Christian experience of every believer, which shine with peculiar lustre to illuminate our pathway, and make the Word of God more precious and better understood. Our entire life should serve but to illuminate that Book of Books — the Bible.

Then why not have a text-meeting, occasionally, in which, with song and prayer, the church may have an opportunity to present such passages from the Bible as have been significantly illuminated by their individual experience? Is there not many a one in the various churches who could present incidents as interesting as that of *S. G.* in connection with his Bible or some of its particular texts, that would prove highly "profitable for reproof, for correction, and for instruction in righteousness?"

And even no more than to give texts that are especially precious to different ones in the church, without any peculiar experience connected with them, would doubtless prove, if held at seasons suitably remote from each other, a highly edifying meeting, and serve to present some of the most significantly helpful passages in the Bible.

"Study it carefully,
 Think of it prayerfully,
Deep in thy heart let its pure precepts dwell!
 Slight not its history,
 Ponder its mystery,
None can e'er prize it too fondly or well.

" Accept the glad tidings,
 The warnings and chidings,
Found in this volume of heavenly lore;
 With faith that's unfailing,
 And love all-prevailing,
Trust in its promise of life evermore.

"With fervent devotion,
 And thankful emotion,
Hear the blest welcome, respond to its call;
 Life's purest oblation,
 The heart's adoration,
Gives to the Saviour, who died for us all.

"May this message of love,
 From the Tribune above,
To all nations and kindreds be given,
 Till the ransomed shall raise
 Joyous anthems of praise—
Hallelujah! on earth and in heaven."

CHAPTER XVII.

A Promise-Meeting.

IN the Bible we find that prayer is a claiming of the promises of God — a pleading of covenanted mercies for His own name's sake. The Bible is full of promises. A Scotchman said he had found thirty-one thousand promises in the Bible! To become familiar with these promises must certainly enrich one's knowledge of the Bible, not merely in the line of the promises, but with regard to the great and prominent doctrines of salvation. But suppose that a Christian should make himself conversant with a thousand promises, not to say thirty-one thousand, what a treasury of divine arguments would such a one have at command to make the basis of his supplications at the throne of mercy. It is because God has "given unto us exceeding great and precious promises," and a high priest who can be touched with the feeling of our infirmities, that we are exhorted to "come boldly unto the throne of grace, that we may obtain mercy, and find grace to help in time of need."

The promises of the Bible are related to our present need, trial and temptation. There is no circumstance in life, whether joyous or sorrowful; there is no emotion whether elevating or depressing; there is no emergency whether helpful or critical; there is, in a word, no possible experience in the life of the Christian, but that in the Bible finds its counterpart and its sustaining promise. And this leads to the discovery that there must be a correspondence between the promises of God and our present need, in order to render them personally and peculiarly applicable and helpful. If the Bible pronounces its beatitude upon the pure in spirit, and promises that they shall see God, then the blessedness of such vision belongs only to the pure in heart, and none but they can claim the promise or find any comfort in it. And so the promises of the Bible are, like the manna, good only for those who appropriate and use them, according to their daily need.

But it is one thing to discover that the Bible is full of promises, and another thing to discover that they are "precious," for it is only as they are thus daily tried and tested, that the discovery of their preciousness is made. And so we are told that a certain Christian wrote on the margin of his Bible by the side of certain of its promises, the letters "P. T." These cabalistic signs, when explained, meant simply that their truth had been proved and tested. O wise and happy Christian thus to test and prove the promises of God (Mal. 3 : 10), for who yet is there from righteous Abel down to the present that has ever tested and proved God to find Him wanting; yea, who yet is there whose experience it is not that "all the promises of God in him are yea, and in him, amen unto the glory of God?" Not one. "He is faithful that promised." "Heaven and earth shall pass away, but my words shall not pass away."

Among the six precious things which Peter writes about in his Epistles, we find that he includes the promises of God. He claims for them two things; first, they are exceeding great, and second they are exceeding precious. If we examine what are the six things which he writes about as being precious, we shall find them to be these: (1) The trial of your faith is precious; (2) the blood of Christ is precious; (3) Christ as a living stone is precious; (4) Christ is precious to those that believe; (5) faith is precious; (6) the promises are precious. And we may well see why Peter should be almost the only New Testament writer to use the word "precious." He had been sorely tried and tempted, and had grievously fallen; and how could he better strengthen the brethren than by exalting Christ, and showing from his own experience that in all those enumerated things he had found them "precious." Would it not be advisable then to arrange for two or three promise-meetings each year, when the various attendants upon our prayer-meetings might have the opportunity to repeat those promises from the Word of God which they have "proved and tested," and by a blessed experience found to be "exceeding precious?" If we had, say two promise-meetings each year, and at each meeting fifty promises were presented that had been especially blessed in the experience of those presenting them, then at this rate it would take three hundred and ten years of prayer-meetings before we could get once through in presenting as many promises as the Scotchman had found. If your church will only faithfully study the Bible, there is no danger that its promises shall be exhausted in the history of the prayer-meeting during the life of any single generation, or presented so frequently as to become trite and threadbare.

A revival-meeting can be conducted at any time, upon the basis of a promise-meeting, or be adapted to meet the spiritual requirements of all present at such a meeting. There are promises that apply to the sinner, such as John 6: 37; to the backslider, Jer. 3: 22; to the believer, Is. 41: 10, 13; and Rev. 21: 4. Are there not times in the history of every church when it would be highly judicious to meet and pray over the promise contained in II. Chron. 7: 14. 15?

" Precious promise God hath given
   To the weary passer-by,
On the way from earth to heaven,
   'I will guide thee with mine eye.'

When temptations almost win thee,
   And thy trusted watchers fly,
Let this promise ring within thee,
   'I will guide thee with mine eye.'

When thy secret hopes have perished,
   In the grave of years gone by,
Let this promise still be cherished,
   'I will guide thee with mine eye.'

When the shades of life are falling,
   And the hour has come to die,
Hear thy trusty pilot calling,
   'I will guide thee with mine eye.' "

CHAPTER XVIII.

An Experience-Meeting.

WE have many passages in the Bible which appeal directly to the experience of the believer, such as, "If any man will do His will, he shall know of the doctrine, whether it be of God, or whether I speak of myself." There are others, also, that appeal to the experience of the unbeliever, such as "Their rock is not as our rock, even our enemies themselves being judges."

"Religious experience," some one has written, "is not like hurdle-racing, where you meet the obstacle plump in your path, gather your powers up for a mighty effort and take it all flying, and then are over it, and done with it. It is more like going up-stairs. You take one step at a time, and so you get up gradually. You cannot get up to the upper rooms in the temple of divine truth and life with a jump. Experiencing religion is an accumulative experience. Its joys come to man as the joy of wider vision comes to the tourist as he climbs a mountain. He gets expansion of view foot by foot, one step at a time, and with effort." Whosoever heareth these sayings of mine and doeth them, I will liken him unto a wise man which built his house upon a rock."

An experience-meeting, at convenient intervals, might be held, for the comfort of faith and the strengthening of hope, in which testimony might be taken on such points as, Finding Christ, Following Christ, The faithfulness of Christ, The method of Christian growth, The blessings of trials, The rewards of Christian work, The joys of Christian life, etc.

Nor would it be out of place, if the published utterances of the opponents of Christianity were brought into court to witness to their experience, that we might see just what no religion is calculated to do for man in life and death, and what its universal prevalence would do for mankind. Infidelity has nothing positive to offer in the place of faith, hope, and charity. It is the science of nescience. A negation is a poor crumb to substitute for the bread and water of eternal life. Thus, Col. Ingersoll has said, "I don't know what I believe. I can tell you all day what I don't believe." Their house most surely is built upon the shifting sands. We may love the colonel, personally, whilst we deprecate his irreligious sentiments. We may admire his genius, the exuberance of his fancy, and the flights of his imagination, whilst we deplore the fruit and tendency of his published teachings. Said Ingersoll, on

May 26, 1876, at the funeral of his father-in-law, just before leaving the house, "Without assurance and without fear we give him back, as it were, to Nature, the Source and Mother of us all. Friend, husband, father, fare thee well!" And at the open grave, he said, "With morn, with noon, with night, with changing clouds and changeless stars — with grass, with trees and birds, with leaf and bud, with flower and blossoming vine, with all the sweet influences of Nature, we leave our dead. Again, farewell!"

Upon the sudden death of his brother in Washington, D. C., he remarked, "Life is a narrow vale, between the cold and barren peaks of two eternities. We strive in vain to look beyond the heights. We cry aloud, and the only answer is the echo of our wailing cry. From the voiceless lips of the unreplying dead there comes no word, but in the night of death, hope sees a star, and listening love can hear the rustle of a wing."

And still later in a recent address, delivered in Cincinnati, Sept. 14, 1879, he observed, "I would wish that the friends who bid us 'good night' in this world, might meet us with 'good morning' there. Just as long as we love one another, we'll hope for another world; just as long as love kisses the lips of death, will we believe and hope for another world."

All must admit that a positive hope is a great gain

even for this life. How this is so, Mr. Moody in the following remarks has shown with telling effect, and from them we may gather some hints for conducting a meeting of this kind. "You know, in the first place," he has said, "that the atheist does not believe in any God. He denies the existence of a God. Now, I contend that his 'rock is not as our rock,' and will let those atheists be the judges. What does an atheist look forward to? Nothing. He is taking a very crooked path in this world. His life has been dark; it has been full of disappointments. When he was a young man, ambition beckoned him on to a certain height. He has attained to that height, but he is not satisfied. He climbs a little higher, and perhaps he has got as far as he can get, but he is not contented. He is dissatisfied, and if he takes a look into the future, he sees nothing. Man's life is full of trouble. Afflictions are as numerous as the hairs of our head, but when the billows of affliction are rising and rolling over him, he has no God to call upon; therefore, I contend his 'rock is not as our rock.' Look at him. He has a child. That atheist has all the natural affection for that child possible. He has a son — a noble young man — who starts out in life full of promise, but he goes astray. He has not the will-power of his father, and cannot resist the temptation of the world. That father cannot call upon God to save his son. He sees that son go down to ruin step by step, and by-and-by he plunges into a hopeless, godless, Christless grave. And as the father looks into that grave, he has no hope. His 'rock is not as our rock.'

"Look at him again. He has a child laid low with fever, racked with pain and torture, but the poor atheist cannot offer any consolation to that child. As he stands by the bedside of that child, she says:

"'Father, I am dying; in a little while I will go into another world. What is going to become of me? Am I going to die like a dumb beast?'

"'Yes,' the poor atheist says, 'I love you, my daughter; but you will soon be in the grave and eaten up with the worms, and that will be all. There is no heaven, no hereafter; it is all a myth. People have been telling you there is a hereafter, but they have been deluding you.'

"Did you ever hear an atheist going to his dying children and telling them this? My friends, when the hour of affliction comes, they call in a minister to give consolation. Why don't the atheist preach no hereafter, no heaven, no God, in the hour of affliction? This very fact is an admission that 'their rock is not as our rock, even our enemies themselves being the judges.'

"But look again. That little child dies, and that

atheist father follows the body to the grave, and lays it down in its resting-place, and says:

"'All that is left of my child is there; it will soon become the companion of worms, who will feed upon it. That is all there is.'

"Why, the poor man's heart is broken, and he will admit his 'rock is not as our rock.'

"A prominent atheist went to the grave with the body of his friend. He pronounced a eulogy, and committed all that was left of his friend to the winds — to nature — and bade the remains farewell forever. Oh, my friends, had he any consolation then? His 'rock was not as our rock.'

"A good many years ago there was a convention held in France, and those who held it wanted to get the country to deny a God, to burn the Bible — wanted to say that a man passed away like a dog — like a dumb animal. What was the result? Not long after, that country was filled with blood. Did you ever think what would take place if we could vote the Bible, and the ministers of the Gospel, and God out from among the people? My friends, the country would be deluged with blood. Your life and mine would not be safe in this city to-night. We could not walk through these streets with safety. We don't know how much we owe God, and the influence of His Gospel, among even ungodly men. I can imagine some of you saying, 'Why this talk about atheists? There are none here.' Well, I hope there isn't; but I find a great number who come into the inquiry-rooms, just to look on, who confess they don't believe in any God or any hereafter.

"But there is another class called deists, who, you know, don't believe in revelation — who don't believe in Jesus Christ. Ask a deist who is his God?

"'Well,' he will say, 'He is the beginning — He who caused all things.'

"'These deists say there is no use to pray, because nothing can change the decrees of their deity; God never answers prayer. 'Their rock is not as our rock.' In the hour of affliction they, too, send off for some Christian to administer consolation.

"But there is another class. They say, I am no deist; I am a pantheist; I believe that God is in the air; He is in the sun, the stars, in the rain, in the water — they say God is in this wood. Why, a pantheist the other night told me God was in that post; he was in the floor. When we come to talk to those pantheists, we find them no better than the deists and atheists. There was one of that sort that Sir Isaac Newton went to talk to. He used to argue with him, and try to get the pantheist into his belief, but he couldn't. In the hour of his distress, however, he cried out to the God of Sir Isaac Newton. Why don't they cry to their God in the hour of their trouble? When I used to be in this city, I used to be called on to attend a good many funerals. I would inquire what the man was in his belief. If I found out he was an atheist, or a deist, or a pantheist, when I would go to the funeral, and in the presence of his friends said one word about that man's doctrine, they would feel insulted. Why is it that, in a trying hour, when they have been talking all the time against God — why is it that in the darkness of affliction, they call in believers in that God to administer consolation?

"The next class I want to call attention to is the infidel. I contend his 'rock is not as our rock.' Look at an infidel. An infidel is one who don't believe in the inspiration of Scripture. These men are very numerous, and they feel insulted when we call them infidels; but the man who don't believe in the inspirations of Scripture is an infidel. A good many of them are in the church, and not a few of them have crept into the pulpit. These men would feel insulted if we called them infidels, but if a man says — I don't care who he is, or where he preaches — if he tries to say that the Bible is not inspired from back to back, he is an infidel. That is their true name, although they don't like to be called that.

"Now in that blessed book there are five hundred or six hundred prophecies, and every one of them has been fulfilled to the letter; and yet men say they cannot believe the Bible is inspired. As I said the other night, those who cannot believe it have never read it. I hear a great many infidels talk against the Bible, but I haven't found the first man who ever read the Bible from back to back carefully, and remained an infidel.

"My friends, the Bible of our mothers and fathers is true. How many men have said to me, 'Mr. Moody, I would give the world if I had your faith, your consolation, the hope you have from your religion.' Is not that a proof that 'their rock is not as our rock?' Now look at those prophecies in regard to Nineveh, in regard to Babylon, to Egypt, to the Jewish nation, and see how literally they have been fulfilled to the letter. Every promise God makes He carries out.

"But although infidels prefer their disbelief in the inspiration of Scripture, they do not believe in their hearts what they declare, else why, when we talk with them, if they have any children, do they send them out of the room? Now, not long ago, I went into a man's house, and when I commenced to talk about religion, he turned to his daughter, and said:

"'You had better go out of the room; I want to say a few words to Mr. Moody.'

"When she had gone, he opened a perfect torrent of infidelity upon me.

"'Why,' said I, 'did you send your daughter out of the room before you said this?'

"'Well,' he replied, 'I did not think it would do her any good to hear what I said.'

"My friends, his 'rock is not as our rock.' Why did he send his daughter out of the room if he believed what he said? It was because he did not believe it. Why, if I believed in infidelity, I would wish my daughters and my sons, my wife, and all belonging to me, sharers in the same belief. I would preach it wherever I went. But they doubt what they advocate. If they believed it down in their souls, why, when their daughters die, do they send for a true Christian to administer consolation? Why don't they send for some follower of Voltaire, or Hume, or Paine? Why, when they make their last will, do they send for some Christian to carry it out? My friends, it is because their rock has no foundation; it is because in the hour of adversity, in spite of all their boasts of the grandeur of infidelity, they cannot trust their infidel friends. 'Their rock is not as our rock, even our enemies themselves being judges.'

"Now, did you ever hear of a Christian in his dying hour recanting? You never did. Did you ever hear of Christians regretting that they had accepted Christianity, and in their dying hour embracing infidelity? I would like to see the man who could stand and say he had. But how many times have Christians been called to the bedside of an atheist, or deist, or infidel, in his dying hours, and heard him crying for mercy? In that hour infidelity is gone, and he wants the God of his father and mother to take the place of his black infidelity.

"It is said of Gilbert West, an eminent man, that he was going to take up the doctrine of the resurrection, and show the world what a fraud it was; while Lord Lyttleton was going to take up the conversion of Saul, and just show the folly of it. These men were going to annihilate that doctrine, and that incident of the Gospel. They were going to emulate the Frenchman who said it took twelve fishermen to build up Christ's religion, but one Frenchman pulled it down. From Calvary this doctrine rolled along the stream of time, through the eighteen hundred years down to. us, and West got at it and began to look at the evidence; but instead of being able to cope with it, he found it perfectly overwhelming — the proof that Christ had risen, that He had come out of the sepulchre, and ascended to heaven, and led captivity captive. The light dawned upon him, and he became an expounder of the Word of God, and a champion of Christianity.

"And Lord Lyttleton, that infidel and sceptic, hadn't been long at the conversion of Saul before the God of Saul broke upon his sight, and he, too, began to preach. I don't believe there is a man in the audience who, if he will take his Bible and read it, but will be convinced of its truth. What does infidelity do for a man?

"'Why,' said a dying infidel, 'my principles have lost me my friends; my principles have sent my wife to her grave with a broken heart; they have made my children beggars, and I go down to my grave without peace or consolation.'

"I have never heard of an infidel going down to his grave happily. But not only do they go on without peace, but how many youths do they turn away from God? How many young men are turned away from Christ by these infidels? Let them remember that God will hold them responsible if they are guilty of turning men away from heaven. A few infidels gathered around a dying friend lately, and they wanted him to hold on to the end, to die like a man. They were trying to cheer him, but the poor infidel turned to them:

"'Ah,' said he, 'what have I got to hold on to?'

"My friends, let me ask you what you have got to hold on to? Every Christian has Christ to hold on to —

the resurrected man. 'I am he that liveth and was dead; and behold, I am alive forevermore.' Thank God, we have some one to carry us through all our trials. But what has the infidel got to hold on to; what hope has the atheist, deist, or pantheist? His gods are false gods.

"They are like the false gods of the Hebrews; they never hear their cry. Whereas, if we have the God of Daniel, of Abraham, He is always ready to succor us when in distress, and we can make Him our fortress, and we have a refuge in the storm of adversity. There we can anchor safely, free from danger and disaster. I was reading to-night almost the last words of Lord Byron, and I want to draw a comparison between the sorrowful words of Byron and those of St. Paul. He died very young — he was only thirty-six — after leading an ungodly life:

"'My days are in the yellow leaf,
  The flower and fruit of life are gone;
 The worms, the canker and the grief
  Are mine alone.'

"Compare those words with the words of St. Paul. 'I have fought a good fight, I have finished my course, I have kept the faith. Henceforth there is laid up for me a crown of righteousness which the Lord the rightous Judge shall give me at that day.' What a contrast!

What a difference! My friends, there is as much difference between them as there is between heaven and hell, between death and life. Be judges, which is the most glorious — atheism, deism, infidelity, or the Christianity of St. Paul. May God take all these isms, and sweep them from the world."

CHAPTER XIX.

A Consecration-Meeting.

WHILST every religious meeting is in one sense a consecration-meeting, yet a meeting with this as its distinctive theme, would undoubtedly place consecration before the mind as an object of more earnest search and intense aspiration. To be sure, the public profession of religion is itself an act of consecration. We tacitly confess it to be our standing duty to live above the world, whilst we live in the world, and to use all things as not abusing them. Whilst all this is true, yet the Christian may grow cold and neglectful of his spiritual interests. It is often the case that the spirit of worldliness in the business competitions, and amid the manifold temptations of life, roll in upon us like a flood. By a meeting of this kind, we should seek to emphasize the reasons, and present the motives for making nearness to God in daily walk, the growing purpose of our life.

I well remember how near God and the spiritual world appeared to be to me, after a week of prayer, preparatory to the coming of Whittle and Bliss, in

1876. to labor in services of revival among our city churches, as well as the deep feeling those initial meetings of consecration produced, when the brethren sought the blessings of God's reviving grace, by confession of sin and earnest supplications for pardon and acceptance. The affairs of this world seemed truly of minor and almost trifling importance, and eternity with its vast concerns, loomed up like Teneriffe, grand and imposing.

An intense longing for souls filled our hearts, and a tender regard for the salvation of all our citizens stirred up the deepest feelings within us, and opened up even the fountain of tears. Had God come in all the majesty and grandeur of a judgment day, it would have occasioned no surprise, but on the contrary, it would have been an event entirely in keeping with our wrought-up emotions.

The exercises in a meeting of this kind as relate to song, Scripture, prayer, remark, the narration of experience, and voluntary parts, should all tend in the one direction of self-consecration — "Nearer my God to Thee, Nearer to Thee."

1. PRAYER.
2. SONG —

"Gracious Spirit! Love divine!
Let Thy light within me shine;

All my guilty fears remove,
Fill me with Thy heavenly love.

Speak Thy pard'ning grace to me,
Set the burdened sinner free;
Lead me to the Lamb of God,
Wash me in His precious blood.

Life and peace to me impart,
Seal salvation on my heart;
Breathe Thyself into my breast,
Earnest of immortal rest.

Let me never from Thee stray,
Keep me in the narrow way;
Fill my soul with joy divine,
Keep me, Lord! forever Thine."

3. SCRIPTURE LESSON — Romans 12th chapter.
4. PRAYER.
5. SONG —

"Oh, happy day that fixed my choice,
On Thee, my Saviour and my God!
Well may this glowing heart rejoice,
And tell its raptures all abroad.

Oh, happy bond that seals my vows,
To Him who merits all my love!
Let cheerful anthems fill His house,
While to that sacred shrine I move.

'Tis done — the great transaction's done;
I am my Lord's and He is mine;

He drew me and I followed on,
    Rejoiced to own the call divine.

Now rest, my long-divided heart!
    Fixed on this blissful centre, rest;
Here have I found a noble part,
    Here heavenly pleasures fill my breast.

High heaven, that hears the solemn vow,
    That vow renewed, shall daily hear;
Till in life's latest hour I bow,
    And bless in death a bond so dear."

6. REMARKS — On the meaning of Ex. 32: 29.
7. PRAYER.
8. VOLUNTARY PARTS.
9. SONG —

"Jesus, my Saviour! bind me fast
    In cords of heavenly love;
Then sweetly draw me to Thy breast,
    Nor let me thence remove.

Draw me from all created good,
    From self, the world and sin,
To the dear fountain of Thy blood,
    And make me pure within.

Oh, lead me to Thy mercy-seat,
    Attract me nearer still;
Draw me, like Mary, to Thy feet,
    To sit and learn Thy will.

> Oh, draw me by Thy providence,
> Thy Spirit and Thy Word,
> From all the things of time and sense
> To Thee, my gracious Lord."

10. REMARKS — On Rom. 12 : 1, 2.
11. PRAYER.
12. SONG —

> "And must I part with all I have,
> My dearest Lord for Thee?
> It is but right, since Thou hast done
> Much more than this for me.
>
> Ten thousand worlds, ten thousand lives,
> How worthless they appear,
> Compared with Thee, supremely good,
> Divinely bright and fair.
>
> Saviour of souls, while I from Thee,
> A single smile obtain,
> Though destitute of all things else,
> I'll glory in my gain."

13. REMARKS — On Col. 3; 2.
14. PRAYER.
15. VOLUNTARY PARTS.
16. SONG —

> "Forth in Thy name, O Lord! I go,
> My daily labor to pursue,
> Thee, only Thee, resolved to know,
> In all I think, or speak, or do.

Give me to bear Thine easy yoke,
  And every moment watch and pray,
And still to things eternal look,
  And hasten to Thy glorious day.

Fain would I still for Thee employ,
  Whate'er Thy boundless grace hath given,
And run my course with even joy.
  And closely walk with Thee to heaven.

17. BENEDICTION.

CHAPTER XX.

A Thanksgiving Prayer-Meeting.

IT has seemed to me to be profitable to hold a Thanksgiving service on the prayer-meeting evening, preceding this annual holiday, in which the parts shall be mainly conducted by the people themselves. The people may have one class of reasons for thankfulness, and the pastor another. There is a large amount of latent happiness in the air just about Thanksgiving time. Think of all that are happy in the land. While there are many sad hearts and many sorrowing ones, yet their number is comparatively small when considered as individual factors, in that vast population of forty million souls dwelling in this land. The majority of the people are rejoicing; and even sorrowing ones have cause to be thankful that their condition is not worse than it is. Think of the many happy family reunions that take place during the recurrence of this stated festival. Think of the children — and how many millions there are — whose hearts are free from care and full of joy; and all this, because Thanksgiving has come round once more.

"The Lord reigneth, let the earth rejoice." Let the people, then, have an opportunity to express their various reasons for grateful thanks, in connection with praise and prayer. Let the people have Wednesday night, and on Thursday morning the pastor can have his opportunity to deepen the interest already created, and strike a cheerful key in the volume and spirit of rejoicing, that shall ascend like incense to the throne of Almighty God. By this method it will be found that there is a greater aggregate, and a greater variety, of reasons for thankfulness, than if one person alone undertook to express them.

For several years past I have been in the habit of holding such services, and I have found them to be not only interesting, and helpful to the production of thankfulness, but also exceedingly precious. For instance, on Wednesday evening, Nov. 28, 1877, I held such a service. On Wednesday evening, Nov. 27, 1878, our subject for the Thanksgiving prayer-meeting was this, "Reasons for Thankfulness;" Eph. 5: 20; and our subject for a similar meeting this year is, "The Blessings of the Year;" Ps. 65.

Let us take the subject, "Reasons for Thankfulness," in order to give a brief illustration. One speaker, for instance, may present a general reason for thankfulness, such as the progress and improvement of mankind.

There are divine forces at work in history, hastening the civilization and evangelization of the world. Look at the gains in the missionary world.

Another speaker may observe that we ought to be thankful for the tokens of returning prosperity vouchsafed unto us as a people. The crops have been abundant, and are now ingathered. The indications favor better times in the near future than have been witnessed during the last twenty years. To be sure, there is an apparent exception to the spirit of thankfulness as found in that calamity that has afflicted the South this year. During the prevalence of the yellow fever, multitudes have been carried away, and many households broken up that at the beginning of the year were united and happy. But even the storm cloud has its lining of silver. We may be thankful that its ravages have been limited, and that they have been accompanied by such acts of heroism as those have manifested who watched by the side of the dying, and also that such streams of charity have flowed in from the whole world for the relief of the sufferers. "One touch of nature makes the whole world kin." May we not hope for more friendly feelings and intimate relations to spring up between the North and the South.

A third person may remark upon reason of thankfulness as found in the peaceful state of public affairs —

no wars with foreign states, nor civil strifes at home — as found in the prosperity of our State, and for the health and growth of our city.

Another speaker may profitably present the spiritual condition of the church, and the reasons for gratitude in connection with its permanence and increase.

A fifth speaker may give thanks that individual life has been spared, and that those present have enjoyed, during the year, so many opportunities for doing good and getting good.

And a last speaker may present some additional reasons for gratitude, in looking at the "bright side" of things, and urge his hearers to cultivate a cheerful religion and a thankful spirit. Let us give "thanks always for all things unto God and the Father, in the name of our Lord Jesus Christ."

The pastor, or leader, in closing the meeting, may briefly sum up the chief lines of thought that have been presented, and urge his hearers not to forget the poor, for whom nothing has been prepared, (Neh. 8: 10). And even though adversity may have been our lot, yet let us joy and rejoice in the God of our salvation; for in Him shall we all eventually be enriched. (Hab. 3: 17-19). Who does not perceive that the minister will be greatly helped by a service like this, of prayer, praise, and thanksgiving, in his own preparation for the more public exercises of Thanksgiving Day?

And now, I am glad that I have at hand the outline of such a service — the people's service — for Thanksgiving Day, as held in the "Fourteenth Street Presbyterian Church, New York city, Rev. F. H. Marling, pastor, on Thursday, Nov. 28, 1878."

In a note to this circular, as sent to me, it was stated that the "People's Service" began "at 11 o'clock, A. M., and closed at 12.20." This plan will serve as a useful hint to the leader, in preparing an outline of parts for the "Wednesday evening, Thanksgiving prayer-meeting." As is evident, the reading of the proclamations should be omitted, and reserved for Thursday morning, and such other parts as would introduce more opportunities for prayer, and reduce the exercises to the limits of an hour. The plan explains itself, and is printed in full:

PEOPLE'S SERVICE.

[*The several parts of this Service will proceed in the following order without announcement at the time. The Readings are from the "Selections for Chanting," at the end of the Hymn Book.*]

1. ANTHEM OF PRAISE . . . . . . *Choir.*
2. RESPONSIVE READING — Selection 37 . *Pastor and Cong'n.*
3. READING of President's Proclamation *H. E. Crampton, M.D.*
4. READING of Governor's Proclamation *R. McMurray, M.D.*

A THANKSGIVING PRAYER-MEETING.

5. HYMN — 1329, verses 1 and 2 . . . *Choir and Cong'n.*
6. GOD'S CALL to Thanksgiving . . . . *The Pastor.*
7. THANKSGIVING in Prayer . . . . . *The Pastor.*
8. THANKSGIVING in Song — Hymn 118, to " Spanish Hymn " . . . . *Choir and Cong'n.*
9. THE BEAUTY of a Thankful Spirit . . *H. E. Rowland.*
10. THE SHAME of Unthankfulness . . *Alex. F. Denniston.*
11. READING in Unison of the Te Deum — Sel. 49.
    Pastor and Cong'n.
12. OUR GROUNDS for Thanksgiving as Citizens *F. H. Wiswell.*
13. READING in Unison of Hymn 1312 . . . *S. S. School.*
14. HYMN 1336, verses 1, 3 and 4 . . . *Choir and Cong'n.*
15. GRATITUDE for Temporal Benefits to the Church *S. Cutter.*
16. REJOICING as " One in Christ," in Prayer *E. P. Walling.*
17. SPECIAL TRIBUTE of Thanksgiving. From " Our Young People ". . . . . *F. H. O. Marling*
18. RECITATION of Hymn . . . . " *The Infantry.*"
19. THANKSGIVING and Thanksliving . . . *F. A. Ferris.*
20. THANK-OFFERING, for the Poor
    "*Every Man as he may be able.*"
21. DOXOLOGY . . . . . . *Choir and Cong'n.*
22. BENEDICTION . . . . *The Pastor.*

CHAPTER XXI.

Moody's Praise Prayer-Meeting.

I WANT to take for my subject to-night "Praise." We spoke at the noon day meeting upon the subject of "Thanksgiving." Now praise is a step in advance of thanksgiving. If you receive blessings from a man, you may thank him, yet you may not praise him. Now praise is not only speaking to the Lord on our own account, but it is praising Him for what He has done for others. We have had a great many prayers going up in this Tabernacle during the past eight weeks for others, and hundreds — I may say thousands — of them have been answered. We should give praise for this. We have in our churches a great deal of prayer, but I think it would be a good deal better if we had a praise-meeting, occasionally. If we could only get people to praise God for what He has done, it would be a good deal better than asking Him continually for something. We like to have our children ask us for things, but if they keep on asking without giving thanks, we become discouraged. Bear this in mind. God expects us to praise Him for what He has done, and if our heart is full of gratitude, and we will praise the Lord, He will do a great deal more for us. And I want to say here, a praise-church is what the Lord wants now.

A cold church — a church that is full of formalism — will never be full of praise; but a church that is full of joy, full of gladness, is praising God all the time.

"Restore unto me the joys of thy salvation, and uphold me with thy free Spirit, then will I teach transgressors thy ways." It seems to me that if we had that text all over Christendom at the present time, the ministers holding it up to the people till the church is filled with peace, till it is filled with rest, till it is filled with gladness, with promise — it seems to me that we would then see a revival as lasting as eternity itself.

Now, as I said one night here before, the world is after the best thing. If a man wants to buy a horse, he goes where he can get the best horse for his money. If a woman wants to get a dress, she will hunt till she gets the very best she can. Why, I have heard of a woman going for half a day, from store to store, to get the best piece of ribbon she could. It's a universal law — the world wants to get the very best thing it can.

Now, if we can show the world that the religion of Jesus Christ is the best thing in it, the world will take it; but if we are despondent or cast down, look gloomy are not full of praise, if we are not full of joy, the world will not want it. We will only drive men out of the kingdom of God. If we have a praise-church, we will have people converted. I don't care where it is, what part of the world it is in; if we have a praise-church, we'll have a successful Christianity.

A young man went down to a church in the East, the pastor of which had become an old man. The people got asleep. The new man came and tried to rouse them, but it was no use. He preached and preached, and tried to get them aroused and go into the prayer-meeting, but he could not. One night he said:

"The next night we'll have no prayer-meeting."

They wondered what it meant; the idea that this young minister should do away with their prayer-meeting, which they had had for fifty years! They were astonished.

"But," said he, "we will have a praise-meeting."

At the close of the meeting, one elder went to another:

"What's he going to give up the prayer-meeting for? Has he consulted you about it?"

"No."

"Well," replied the former, "that's a very serious matter; what's the meaning of a praise-meeting?"

They had been going along without any praise-meeting, and they did not know what a praise-meeting meant! They went to ask him, but he wouldn't tell them, but said, wait till next Friday night, and then they would see. They began to talk about it, and out of curiosity a great many came to see what it was. The young minister read some of those good old psalms, that are full of praise.

"Now," said he, "if you can think of anything in your past life that you have received from God, praise God to-night for it. You have been asking God for everything, and it chills the church through. Now if you can think of any benefits you have received, praise God for them."

They began to think, and they found they had a good many things to praise God for. One man got up and praised God for a praying mother, who had led him to Christ. Another man got up and praised God for the Bible. Another praised God for this and that, and the result was that when the meeting was over, instead of getting up and walking out, they stopped and shook hands with one another, and spoke to one another, and said:

"I believe we are going to have a revival."

My friends, if we don't thank God for what He has done for us, and be full of joy and gladness, the world will not come to Christ. Would to God that we had a praise-church all over Christendom. Let Christ's name be in the churches. Let them praise Him for what He has done, and the world will come. Let the world know that this is the name in which we trust, that this is the name we speak well of; and when His disciples begin to do this, then the world will realize the goodness of His Gospel. Thank God, the people of Chicago begin to talk about Christ; and if we can get men to talk about Christ in the steam-cars, in the places of business, in the horse-cars, in the streets — if we can get them to talk about Christ and His loveliness, it won't be long before thousands are converted in a day. May God awaken the Christians to praise Him for what He has done.

Did you ever stop to think that the heart of man is the only thing that does not praise the Lord? The heavens declare His glory; the sun praises Him; the moon and stars praise Him. As the rain falls from heaven it praises God; all nature praises God; the very dumb creatures give Him praise, and it is only the heart of man that won't praise Him. Oh, how deceitful is the heart of man. He who gets the most temporal blessings is the man that praises God least. A man may be thankful for those blessings, yet he does not praise Him. In fact, I don't believe that any man can praise God till he is born of God. You may be thankful for His blessings, but praising Him is another thing; praise is the occupation of heaven. Those people who do not praise God here, I don't know what they will do when they get into heaven; they will be strangely out of place there, because that is the occupation of heaven. The redeemed, praise Him all the time.

There was a little boy converted, and he was full of praise. When God converts man or boy he is full of joy — can't help praising. His father was a professed Christian. The boy wondered why he didn't talk about Christ, and didn't go down to the special meetings. One day, as the father was reading the papers, the boy came to him, and put his hand on his shoulder, and said:

"Why don't you praise God? Why don't you go down to these meetings that are being held?"

The father opened his eyes, and looked at him, and said gruffly:

"I am not carried away with any of those doctrines. I am established."

A few days after they were out getting a load of wood. They put it on the cart. The father and the boy got on top of the load, and tried to get the horse to go. They used the whip, but the horse wouldn't move. They got off and tried to roll the wagon along, but they could neither move wagon nor horse.

"I wonder what's the matter?" said the father.

"He's established," replied the boy.

You may laugh at that, but this is the way with a good many Christians. The reason is, that they are not born of God, or else they have got so far away that they don't exactly know where they are.

Now, if we are really born of God, if the heart is really filled with the Spirit of God, we cannot help praising Him. I pity the Christian that has no praise in his heart. You are living a life of formalism — you are living on doctrines. You haven't got Christ in your soul, if you don't praise Him. Now, that ought to be the text. Ask yourself, have you praised God this peaceful day of Thanksgiving? You say:

"Oh, yes, I've thanked Him."

But have you spoken well of Christ? Have you spoken well of what He has done? Have you sung "hallelujah! hallelujah!" for these six months or a year, for this is what they sing in heaven.

If a man is born of God, he can't help praising God. Fill this building with young converts, and see how they will sing:

"Oh, happy day, happy day, when Jesus washed my sins away."

They cannot hear such songs without praising God.

The first impulse of a young convert is to praise, and if he don't feel like praising the God who saved him, it is a true sign that he has not been converted by the grace of God; he has been born to some creed or profession, some man or some church, and not to the loving Son of God, because when Christ comes into the heart, He brings joy.

Now, take a servant of the devil, he don't praise. Fill this building full of unregenerated men, and try to get them to sing praises. You can't do it; their mouths are sealed; there is no praise in their heart. But you get this building filled with men with the Lord Jesus Christ in their hearts, they cannot help praising Him. How can a man whose master is the devil, praise him? Have you ever heard a man rejoice in his service? I never heard one.

Now a great many of you say, " It is all very well for him to stand up there and talk about praise. If I was in a comfortable condition, good health, and everything I wanted, like a good many others I see, I would praise God."

It is circumstances with a good many, but I have found people who were poor in this world's goods, in bad health, and yet continually praising God. I can take you to a poor burdened one, who has not been off her bed for ten years, and yet she praises Him more than hundreds of thousands of Christians. Her chamber seems to be just the ante-room of heaven. Her soul is full of the love of God, full of gladness, and she is poor. Like Elijah at the brook Cherith, she is just fed by the Almighty; God provides for all her wants.

Any man who knows God, can trust Him and praise Him. He knows that the Word of God is true, for he knows that He will care for him. He who cares for the lilies of the field, He, without whose knowledge not a sparrow can fall to the ground, He, who knows every hair of our heads — any man who knows all this, cannot but rejoice.

Is there any one here, who, although he is poor, can find no reason to praise God? Some of those Christians who are so poor, but who have the love of God, would not give up their place for that of princes. Now my experience is, that a man who lives nearest to God, praises Him most, whether he is rich or poor. The nearer he gets to heaven, the more he praises Him. The man who is furthest from God, praises Him least. Now, if there is any Christian here who cannot praise God, there is something between him and God, and take my advice and have it removed before you go to bed to-night. What the world wants is joyful Christianity, and if we have not that, we are not going to see a saved world. A backslider cannot see God. Fill this building with backsliders, and see if they will sing praises. That prodigal off there in that foreign land, would sing strangely:

"Rock of Ages, cleft for me."

Do you think that Peter, when he had denied Christ, could sing a song of praise to Him? The moment a man turns his back on God, there is no praise. I think that is the reason there are so many quartette choirs in the churches. The people cannot sing themselves, and they have to hire people to sing for them; give them $4,000 or $5,000 per year to sing the songs of praises.

Look at a church filled with the children of God. The moment a minister gives out the song, their hearts burst with praise; they don't want anybody to sing for them. If they can't sing with their mouths, songs will bubble out of their hearts; but when a man is backslidden he wants artistic sounds, wants fine music to touch his ears; don't want it to affect his heart. Now, Israel could not sing there in Egypt when they were making bricks with straw; they could not sing with the crack of the slave-drivers whip in their ears; but when they got through the Red Sea, they struck up the song of redemption, and when a man is redeemed by the precious blood of Jesus Christ, he cannot help praising

God. Do you know, I believe the devil is very wise in this. He don't want a singing-church, he don't want a praise-church. If we have a praise-church, a singing-church, he knows there will be a good many joining us. He knows that is the native air of heaven, and the moment a child is born in heaven, he catches the enthusiasm.

I am told that once during a campaign, the general of an army forbade the playing of the soldier's native airs, because it made them so homesick and despondent that they could not fight. So when we hear the songs of Zion, we are weaned from this world, and want to go home. We feel that we are pilgrims and strangers here, and we have a better world yonder.

Now, how is it that the church does not praise God more? I tell you I think it is very plain. The trouble is, we have got settled down and gone to sleep. I never heard of a bird that sung in its nest, and I don't believe that any man ever did, and when a church gets settled down, it goes to sleep. It is when the bird is on the wing that it sings; and so it is when the church is up it sings songs of praise. And it can sing in the dark — a nightingale can sing in the dark. Paul and Silas, in the darkness of that Philippian night, sung songs of praise. When they put them into that jail, Almighty God was with them. You know when Joseph went down to Egypt, how God was with him. When they put him in prison, they had to lock God Almighty up with him, and Joseph sung songs of praise. But, my friends, if we are down in Egypt, and have turned our backs on God, and been taken captive, we are dumb. It is only when we have been true to God that we can sing in the darkness.

Now I am told that an English lark never sings when coming down; only when mounting up. That may be true or not, but when a church is coming down, it is not a praise-church. When mounting up, and it knows it is coming nearer and nearer to God, it is full of praise. It cannot help it. When the lark is mounting up, up, up, when it is nearly out of sight, so that you can scarcely see it, it sings sweetest. And so when the Christian is rising up near to Christ, so that you cannot see him, he gives out the sweetest notes of praise from his heart.

Now I can imagine some of you saying, "I have got a good many things going against me. I've got a good many reasons for not praising God."

I find there is no reason in the world why we should not praise God. If we have troubles, if we have sorrows or afflictions, we have brought them upon ourselves. They are only to wean us to God. Every good gift that we have had from the cradle up, has come from God. If a man just stops to think what he has to praise God for, he will find there is enough to keep him singing praises for a week. As the flakes of snow come down from the heavens, so He showers His blessings upon us, and if we praise Him for them, He will bless us more abundantly.

Now, there are people always praising. If you are sick, it is like good medicine to see them. Then there are other people always looking on the dark side. There was a man converted here some years ago, and he was just full of praise. He was living in the light all the time. We might be in the darkness, but he was always in the light. He used to preface everything in the meeting with "praise God." One night he came to the meeting with his finger all bound up. He had cut it, and had cut it pretty bad, too. Well, I wondered how he would praise God for this; but he got up and said:

"I have cut my finger, but, praise God, I didn't cut it off."

And so, if things go against you, just think they might be a good deal worse. A soldier who came from the war always used to say he could tell when a Christian addressed a soldier. One man would say:

"You lost your leg. Where did you lose it?"

"In the army."

"What a pity you ever went into the war," he would reply; "I feel sorry for you."

Another would come along:

"You have lost an arm; have you been in the army?"

"Yes."

"Well, that's a pity; but bless God, you didn't lose the other arm."

There was a man on the North Side, and I never came out of his house without praising God. He was deaf, he was dumb, blind, and had the lockjaw. He had a hole in his tooth, and all the food he took was put through that hole. My friend, do you ever thank God for your senses? Do you ever thank God for your eyes by which you can read His Word?

Think of the three millions of people in this world who haven't any sight at all. Hundreds of thousands of them never saw the mother that gave them birth; never saw their own offspring; never saw nature in all its glory; never saw that beautiful sun and all the stars. Do you ever praise God for the ears by which you can hear the voice of man, by which you hear the Gospel preached; by which you hear the songs of Zion? Did you ever praise Him for your hearing and your reason? Go down to yonder madhouse. I never come out of it without feeling full of praise to God. There you will find fathers and mothers and children without the light of reason.

Now my friends, let us praise God we have a home in this Gospel land. Let us praise God for His blessed Bible. Let us praise God for the gift of his only Son. Let us praise Him that He gave up that Son freely for us all. Let us praise Him to-night for the love of His Son and let us go out of this building with our hearts full of joy.

CHAPTER XXII.

Song Service for the Prayer-Meeting.

IN a meeting of this kind it is designed that the element of song shall largely predominate. A hymn, generally, if not always, is a prayer breathed forth in melody to express the emotions of a thankful, confiding and rejoicing heart. A hymn, generally, is a prayer containing confession, petition, adoration and aspiration. Let no one think, then, if we were to have a service with no other parts but the reading of Scripture the singing of spiritual songs and the benediction, that such a meeting would not be a prayer-meeting, for God's Word is the basis of prayer, and Christian song is the rhythmical expression of prayer, and the apostolic benediction, is prayer.

There are various ways in which this service can be conducted to the spiritual good of the people. There may be times when they are too depressed, or too sorrowful to have much heart for singing. "By the rivers of Babylon, there we sat down: yea, we wept, when we remembered Zion. We hanged our harps upon the willows in the midst thereof. For there they that carried us away captive required of us a song; and they that wasted us required of us mirth, saying, 'Sing us one of the songs of Zion.'"

But there are other times when nothing will so rest and inspire the people as the singing of a series of songs, through which their emotions and aspirations shall find utterance. The psalm, which immediately follows the one from which the above quotation is made, is the expression of such a feeling, and the exact opposite of that mood which refuses to sing. "I will praise thee with my whole heart; before the gods* will I sing praise unto thee. I will worship toward thy holy temple, and praise thy name for thy loving kindness and for thy truth: for thou hast magnified thy word above all thy name. In the days when I cried thou answeredst me, and strengthenedst me with strength in my soul. All the kings of the earth shall praise thee. O Lord, when they hear the words of thy mouth. Yea, they shall sing in the ways of the Lord: for great is the glory of the Lord."

Such seasons may be profitably chosen, at varying intervals during the year, and the three following plans are given as practical hints in this direction:

---

*For the meaning see Ex. 22: 28; Ps, 82: 6; John 10: 34, 36; and I. John 3: 1, 2.

First Method.

There are many hymns which have an interesting history connected with them. They have been composed to commemorate some signal experience, deliverance, or aspiration in religious life. And, besides, the singing of a hymn has often been blessed of the Holy Ghost to the conversion of souls. Histories and anecdotes of this kind have been treasured by the church, which it would be most interesting to present at the prayer-meeting, from time to time, in connection with the singing of such hymns. Accordingly the remarks at such meetings may be chiefly directed to present such facts and incidents as shall illustrate their origin or use.

Valuable assistance for services of this kind will be derived by the pastor and the people from such books as "Hezekiah Butterworth's Story of The Hymns," "The Illustrated History of Hymns," by Rev. E. M. Long; and "Trophies of Song," by Rev. W. F. Crafts. And these remarks may be either before or after the singing of the hymn in question as may seem most desirable. In the following plan I have sketched in outline, some remarks of this nature in connection with four of the hymns that are sung :

1. HYMN —

"Come, Thou Fount of every blessing,
Tune my heart to sing Thy grace;
Streams of mercy never ceasing,
Call for songs of loudest praise."

2. SCRIPTURE LESSON AND PRAYER.
3. HYMN —

"I love to steal awhile away,
From every cumbering care,
And spend the hours of setting day
In humble, grateful prayer."

4. REMARKS upon this hymn that has just been sung. This hymn was composed under the following interesting circumstances: "Along a mountain stream, skirted with trees and alders, near the village of Ellington, Ct., there was a well-trodden footpath that led from a cottage to a place of prayer. Hither, at the close of each day, a mother was wont to wend her way to hold sweet communion with God. On one summer evening she was chided by a neighbor for thus stealing 'awhile away' to the seeming neglect of her family. Being much pained by these words, when she returned home, she sat down and penned this hymn as an answer to the criticism, and named it 'An apology for my twilight rambles, addressed to a lady.' The writer of this hymn was Mrs. Phœbe H. Brown. One of the little ones for whom she was thus accustomed to pray, is now the Rev. Sam'l R Brown, D.D., who has been a most efficient mission-

ary in Japan, since 1859. What an example to praying mothers, and what an apt illustration of God's promises, showing that those who resort to 'the secret place of the most high, shall abide under the shadow of the Almighty —' that when we pray to Him in secret He shall reward us openly. The prayers of this earnest mother were answered in the godly life of all her children."

5. PRAYER.
6. HYMN—

"O Thou that hearest prayer!
Attend our humble cry,
And let Thy servants share
Thy blessings from on high."

7. VOLUNTARY REMARKS or Prayer.
8. HYMN—

"Saviour! visit Thy plantation;
Grant us Lord a gracious rain;
All will come to desolation
Unless Thou return again.
Lord! revive us,
All our help must come from Thee."

9. HYMN—

"There is a fountain filled with blood,
Drawn from Immanuel's veins;
And sinners plunged beneath that flood,
Lose all their guilty stains."

10. REMARKS to explain this hymn as just sung: "This hymn was written by the poet Cowper, for the Olney Cottage prayer-meeting, which was led by him and his friend Newton; but little did Cowper imagine, when he heard Newton announce, and this small praying band unite to sing —

'There is a fountain filled with blood,'

that there was starting a song that would afterwards be caught up by unnumbered millions, and that a century later, while his

——' poor, lisping, stammering tongue
 Lies silent in the grave,'

would still be repeated from the rising to the setting of the sun — and continue to echo round the globe,

''Till all the ransomed Church of God,
 Be saved to sin no more.'

This hymn presents the great doctrine of atonement, — a doctrine that infuriates the heart of a proud and boastful sinner, and that especially provokes the wrath of an Ingersoll, who has vowed to let no public lecture pass without his denunciation of it — but a doctrine most precious to every repenting and believing soul, that but for the vicarious suffering of Christ, would be driven to despair. Numerous instances witness to the power of the truth here contained. A notorious robber of New York grew weary of his sinful life, and wanted to become a Christian, but almost despaired of being saved. A Christian believer talked and prayed with him, but could not give him any encouragement. He then sang the first verse of this hymn, but the poor man said 'There is nothing in that for me.' He then sang the second verse —

'The dying thief rejoiced to see
That fountain in his day;
And there may I though vile as he,
Wash all my sins away."

'That means me,' said the penitent robber. Hope sprung up at once in his heart, and he was soon after most happily converted."

11. PRAYER.
12. HYMN —

"Jesus, lover of my soul!
Let me to Thy bosom fly
While the billows near me roll,
While the tempest still is high."

13. REMARKS — " Charles and John Wesley and Richard Pilmore were holding one of their twilight meetings on the common when the mob assailed them, and they were compelled to flee for their lives. Being separated for a time as they were being pelted with stones, they at length, in their flight, succeeded in getting beyond a hedge row, where they prostrated themselves on the ground, and placed their hands on the back of their heads for protection from the stones, which still came so near that they could feel the current of air made by the missiles as they went whizzing over them. In the night-shades that were gathering, they managed to hide from the fury of the

rabble in a spring-house. Here they struck a light with a flint-stone, and after dusting their clothes, and washing, they refreshed themselves with the cooling water that came bubbling up in the spring, and rolling out in a silver streamlet. Now, it should be remembered that Charles Wesley was a ready writer of hymns, and wrote as many as four thousand in all, and so found inspiration in every circumstance of life. After this escape, he pulled out a lead pencil (made by hammering to a point a piece of lead) and drawing inspiration from these surroundings, composed this noble hymn. Almost every line in the hymn was illustrated by something that had just happened, or was suggested by the shelter they had found from the storm and tempest, by the side of the waters that flowed at their feet. Many are the souls that have been converted through the instrumentality of this hymn, and who shall tell the number of those who, both in life and death, have derived from it a sweet and precious comfort."

14. PRAYER.

15. HYMN—

"Give to the winds thy fears;
   Hope, and be undismay'd;
God hears thy sighs and counts thy tears.
   God shall lift up thy head."

16. REMARKS explanatory —" It was a dark day for Paul Gerhardt when he wrote this hymn. On account of some conflict with the king, in his religious sentiments, he

was ordered to leave the Nicholas Church, at Berlin, where he had preached for ten years, and quit the country. With his helpless wife and little ones he turned his steps toward Saxony, his native land. The journey taken on foot was long and weary, and as they turned aside to spend the night in a little village inn, his wife, overcome with sorrow, gave way to tears of anguish. Gerhardt, concealing his own sadness, quoted the beautiful promise — 'Trust in the Lord; in all thy ways acknowledge Him, and He shall direct thy paths.' His own mind was so impressed by these words, that he turned aside and composed this hymn. Late that evening two men came in, and in a conversation stated that they were going to Berlin to Gerhardt, the deposed minister. His wife turned pale with alarm, but the minister, with entire self-possession, told the strangers he was the man they were seeking. To his joy and surprise, he learned that they were sent with a letter from Duke Christian of Meresburg, to inform him that in view of his unjust deposition he had conferred a pension upon him. With great delight, Gerhardt turned to his wife, and handing her this hymn which had been composed earlier in the evening, when all was so dark and seemingly hopeless, said, 'See how God provides!' Man's extremity is God's opportunity."

17. DOXOLOGY AND APOSTOLIC BENEDICTION.

Second Method.

The following Song Service was held in Brantford, Ontario, on the evening of Nov. 17th, 1878, as a Gospel-meeting, and was conducted by the leader, Rev. Dr. Nichol. Those who attended, speak of it as a most refreshing season, commanding close attention and developing an unusual interest. And those who think that the services of the prayer-meeting ought to be "revivalistic" in their nature, will see that it is not impossible to reach out after the unconverted on this plan, and especially so if such are present. And that it was arranged as a plan, before the meeting was held by Dr. Nichol, is nothing more against it, than it is for an evangelist, or so called revivalist, to premeditate the remarks which shall form the sermon for a given meeting, on a certain text, with the other parts forecast in outline:

OPENING HYMN — "Holy Spirit, Faithful Guide."
READING — Scriptures and Prayer.
GOSPEL Invitation — "Come Unto Me," etc.
SECOND Hymn — "Come to the Saviour."
I. But I am a sinner, how can I come? Luke 5 : 32. Read by S. M. Thomson, with a few words of invitation.
THIRD Hymn — "Just as I am."

II. Is there nothing to do to merit salvation? Ephes. 2:8; Is. 55:1. Responded to by Wm. Garside in a few appropriate words.

FOURTH Hymn — "Jesus paid it all."

III. Is there salvation for me? John 3:16; Rev. 22:17. Replied to by John S. Hardie.

FIFTH Hymn — "Whosoever heareth."

IV. I need a guide. Ps. 48:14. Answered by Thos. Foster.

SIXTH Hymn — "Precious Promise."

V. What provision has God made for me? I. John 3:1 and 2. Reply suitably given by Wm. Geddes.

SEVENTH Hymn — "Still there's more to follow."

RESOLUTION — I will arise. Responded to by the chairman, in a very effective manner.

EIGHTH Hymn — "I am coming to the Cross."

PRAYER and Singing. The Doxology closed this interesting meeting.

Third Method.

This plan has more singing in it, than either of the preceding, and with the explanations accompanying it, is taken from the columns of *The Watchman.* This programme will occupy an hour, allowing one minute for each verse sung, and three to five minutes for remarks on each topic. If the leader prepares a time-table on this basis and finds that there is danger of running over the allotted time, he can omit some of the singing. The hymns are from Gospel Hymns, No. 1:

101 — "All hail the power of Jesus' name."
  PRAYER.
 23 — "Jesus loves even me. Vs. 1, 2.
  READ Rom. iii. 9-26.
  REMARKS — Man's condition — sinful.
 41 — "The whole world was lost." Vs. 1, 3.
127 — "Come ye sinners." Vs. 1, 4.
  REMARKS — God's Remedy — Jesus Christ.
 91 — "There is a fountain." Vs. 1, 2.
 30 — "God loved the world." Vs. 1, 2.
 78 — "One offer of salvation." Vs. 1, 2.
  PRAYER.
  REMARKS — How received — by faith.
  2 — "'Tis the promise of God." Vs. 1, 2, 6.
 94 — "Only trust Him." Vs. 1, 3.
  REMARKS — The result — life and peace.
 80 — "There is life for a look." Vs. 1, 5.
100 — "My heart that was heavy." Vs. 1, 2, 3.
  PRAYER.
132 — "Come to Jesus." Vs. 1, 2, 3.

The leader announces all the hymns and may deliver the addresses, but it is generally better to invite different persons to speak, giving each one a clear idea of his own topic and of its relation to the others. The leader of singing should be furnished with a list of hymns beforehand, that there be no delay in starting them. The singing should be spirited and congregational, with very brief organ interludes, if any. The choir should be composed entirely of Christians, and should simply lead the singing and not make a musical display. There may be a solo, occasionally. All hearts should be directed to the truth sung, not to the manner of its rendering. The meeting is not a class for musical instruction, or for the practice of new pieces. But it takes advantage of the love for music which is so constantly appealed to in worldly entertainments, and so proves attractive to many persons who could hardly be persuaded to attend any other service.

CHAPTER XXIII.

Different Methods for Conducting Bible Readings.

IT has been my purpose to give as great a variety, as might be, in the history of actual meetings, by giving the account of such especially as have attained to the interest of having been written and spoken about. I am indebted to the Rev. I. K. Funk, for the following report of a prayer-meeting which was held in a church in Brooklyn, on the subject of "The Resurrection of Christ," This theme had been announced from the pulpit on the preceding Sabbath.

"My lessons," said the leader, "are all drawn from Scripture texts. The brethren will please turn to the passages of Scripture which I will announce, and signify as quickly as they have found them. You will all find Bibles in your seats. My points are:

"1. The fact of the Resurrection. Matt. 18: 2-6.

"'I have found it,' said a lady not far from the leader's chair.

"'Please keep the place until I call upon you to read it.'

"2. The power of the risen Christ. Matt. 28: 18.

"'I have it,' said a gentleman, near the door.

"3. The great truth to be proclaimed. Acts 17: 18.

"4. The fruits of the Resurrection. I. Pet. 1: 3, 4.

"5. Christ's Resurrection the assurance of our immortality. I. Cor. 15: 20.

"6. The triumphant song of the Christian. I. Cor. 15: 56.

"Now," continued the leader, when all these texts had been found, "will the one who has Matt. 28: 2–6 read?"

The verses were read, and the speaker commented upon them briefly; and then the next passage was read and commented upon, and so to the end. This plan broke up the monotony of the service and made it easy to hold the attention of the audience."

The Rev. M. P. Ormsby, pastor of the Presbyterian Church, at Eureka, Ill., has furnished a good suggestion which may be made the basis of a Bible Reading, from memory. "The week before," he writes, "select twelve or fifteen verses of Scripture, as for a Bible Reading Service. Write each on a little slip of paper, and give them out to such as may like to take them. And at the next prayer-meeting ask for them in order, invite remarks, and yourself make remarks. Most of them will be repeated from memory, and the others read. Let the leader supply the place of such as may be absent.

"This method has been in use among us a few months, and is much liked. It secures much study of the Scriptures, calls out many valuable and suggestive thoughts, and centres the remarks of all upon one general theme. It affords a fine opportunity for the young and timid to take part, and for the sisters, without the violation of the divine rule, to "keep silence in the churches." Children, and young people, generally, like to recite the passages, and listen closely to the remarks upon them. Doubtless, no one way, can well be followed forever; but this will apparently work well a good while."

And for farther varieties of this sort, I beg to refer the reader to Chapter IX. of "The Prayer-Meeting And Its Improvement."

A word, also, may be added just here about methods of reading. The reading of verses from the Bible may be done by the leader, or some one who is a good reader may be asked to read the passages, when called for by the leader, or different ones in the audience may attend to the reading, as previously designated, or finally, the texts may be read by the meeting in concert.

CHAPTER XXIV.

A Watch Prayer-Meeting.

A VERY interesting meeting is held by some churches, especially by M. E. Churches, on the last evening of the year, and continued until the midnight hour, which is called a watch-meeting. I have no doubt but that such meetings for conference, prayer, praise and good resolutions, when properly conducted are valuable means of grace.

An outline of such a meeting will prove as suggestive as anything that might be written, in the way of a more lengthy introduction:

1. Song —

> "While with ceaseless course the sun
> Hasted through the former year,
> Many souls their race have run,
> Never more to meet us here;
> Fixed in an eternal state
> They have done with all below;
> We, a little longer wait,
> But how little none can know.
>
> As the winged arrow flies
> Speedily the mark to find

As the lightning from the skies
　　Darts, and leaves no trace behind,
Swiftly thus our fleeting days
　　Bear us down life's narrow stream;
Upward, Lord! our spirits raise;
　　All below is but a dream.

Thanks for mercies past receive,
　　Pardon of our sins renew;
Teach us henceforth how to live
　　With eternity in view;
Bless Thy Word to young and old,
　　Fill us with a Saviour's love;
And when life's short tale is told
　　May we dwell with Thee above."

2. PRAYER.

3. SONG —

"Great God! we sing Thy mighty hand,
By which supported still we stand;
The opening year Thy mercy shows;
That mercy crowns it till its close.

By day, by night, at home, abroad,
Still we are guarded by our God ·
By His incessant bounty fed
By His unerring counsel led.

With grateful hearts the past we own;
The future all to us unknown,
We to Thy guardian care commit,
And peaceful leave before Thy feet.

In scenes exalted or depressed
Be Thou our joy, and Thou our rest;
Thy goodness all our hopes shall raise,
Adored through all our changing days.

When death shall close our earthly songs,
And seal in silence mortal tongues,
Our helper, God, in whom we trust,
In better worlds our souls shall boast."

4. READ Psalm 90, and Mark 13: 33–37.
5.' PRAYER.
6. A SHORT address.
7. SONG —

"Come let us anew
Our journey pursue,
Roll round with the year
And never stand still till the Master appear;
His adorable will
Let us gladly fulfil
And our talents improve
By the patience of hope and the labor of love.

Our life is a dream ;
Our time, as a stream,
Glides swiftly away,
And the fugitive moment refuses to stay;
The arrow is flown,
The moment is gone,
The millenial year
Rushes on to our view, and eternity's here.

> Oh, that each in the day
> Of His coming may say,
> 'I have fought my way through,
> I have finished the work which Thou gav'st me to do!'
> Oh that each from his Lord
> May receive the glad word,
> 'Well and faithfully done!
> Enter into my joy and sit down on my throne!"

8. READ Thomson's "Hymn on The Seasons."

> "These, as they change, Almighty Father, these
> Are but the varied God. The rolling year
> Is full of Thee. Forth in the pleasing spring
> Thy beauty walks; Thy tenderness and love
> Wide flush the fields; the softening air is balm;
> Echo the mountains round; the forest smiles;
> And every sense and every heart is joy.
> Then comes Thy glory in the summer months,
> With light and heat refulgent. Then Thy sun
> Shoots full perfection through the swelling year;
> And oft Thy voice in dreadful thunder speaks,
> And oft at dawn, deep noon, or falling eve,
> By brooks and groves in hollow — whispering gales.
> Thy bounty shines in autumn unconfined,
> And spreads a common feast for all that lives.
> In winter awful thou! with clouds and storms
> Around the throne, tempest o'er tempest rolled,
> Majestic darkness! On the whirlwind's wing
> Riding sublime, Thou bids't the world adore,
> And humblest nature with Thy northern blast.

Mysterious round! what skill, what force divine,
Deep felt, in these appear! a simple train,
Yet so delightful mixed, with such kind art,
Such beauty and beneficence combined;
Shade, unperceived, so softening into shade;
And all so forming an harmonious whole,
That, as they still succeed, they ravish still.
But wandering oft, with brute unconscious gaze,
Man marks not Thee, marks not the mighty hand,
That, ever busy, wheels the silent spheres;
Works in the secret deep; shoots, steaming thence
The fair profusion that o'erspreads the spring;
Flings from the sun direct the flaming day;
Feeds every creature; hurls the tempest forth;
And, as on earth, this grateful change revolves,
With transport touches all the springs of life.

Nature, attend! join every living soul,
Beneath the spacious temple of the sky,
In adoration join; and ardent, raise
One general song! To Him, ye vocal gales,
Breathe soft, whose Spirit in your freshness breathes:
O, talk of Him in solitary glooms!
Where o'er the rock, the scarcely waving pines
Fills the brown shade with a religious awe,
And ye whose bolder note is heard afar,
Who shake the astonished world, lift high to heaven
The impetuous song, and say from whom you rage.
His praise, ye brooks, attune, ye trembling rills;
And let me catch it, as I muse along.

Ye headlong torrents, rapid, and profound;
Ye softer floods, that lead the humid maze
Along the vale; and thou, majestic main,
A secret world of wonders in thyself —
Sound his stupendous praise — whose greater voice
Or bids you roar or bids your roarings fall.
Soft roll your incense, herbs, and fruits and flowers,
In mingled clouds to Him — whose sun exalts,
Whose breath perfumes you, and whose pencil paints;
Ye forests bend, ye harvests wave, to Him;
Breathe your still song into the reaper's heart
As home he goes beneath the joyous moon.
Ye that keep watch in heaven, as earth asleep
Unconscious lies; effuse your mildest beams
Ye constellations, while your angels strike,
Amid the spangled sky, the silver lyre.
Great source of day! best image here below
Of thy Creator, ever pouring wide
From world to world, the vital ocean round
On Nature write with every beam his praise.
The thunder rolls: be hushed the prostrate world:
While cloud to cloud returns the solemn hymn.
Bleat out afresh, ye hills; ye mossy rocks,
Retain the sound; the broad responsive low,
Ye valleys, raise! for the great Shepherd reigns,
And his unsuffering Kingdom yet will come.
Ye woodlands all awake! a boundless song
Burst from the graves! and when the restless day,
Expiring, lays the warbling world asleep,
Sweetest of birds! sweet Philomela, charm

The listening shades and teach the night his praise.
Ye chief, for whom the whole creation smiles,
At once the head, the heart, and tongue of all
Crown the great hymn! in swarming cities vast,
Assembled men to the deep organ join
The long-resounding voice, oft breaking clear,
At solemn pauses, through the swelling bass :
And, as each mingling flame increases, each,
In one united ardor rise to heaven.
Or if you rather choose the rural shade,
And find a fane in every sacred grove.
There let the shepherd's flute, the virgin's lay,
The prompting seraph, and the poet's lyre,
Still sing the God of seasons as they roll.
For me, when I forget the darling theme,
Whether the blossom blows, the summer ray
Russets the plain, inspiring autumn gleams,
Or winter rises in the blackening east,
Be my tongue mute — my fancy paint no more,
And, dead to joy, forget my heart to beat.

Should fate command me to the farthest verge
Of the green earth, to distant barbarous climes,
Rivers unknown to song — where first the sun
Gilds Indian mountains, or his setting beam
Flames on the Atlantic isles it's naught to me :
Since God is ever present, ever felt
In the void waste as in the city full ;
And where He vital spreads there must be joy
When even at last the solemn hour shall come

And wing my mystic flight to future worlds,
I cheerful will obey! 'twere with new powers,
Will rising wonders sing: I can not go
Where Universal Love not smiles around,
Sustaining all yon orbs and all their suns;
From seeming evil still educing good,
And better thence again, and better still,
In infinite progression. But I lose,
Myself in Him, in light ineffable!
Come, then, Expressive Silence, muse His praise."

9. REFLECTIONS and Experiences.
10. SONG —

"Holy Father! Thou hast taught us
　We should live to Thee alone;
Year by year Thy hand hath brought us
　On through dangers oft unknown.
When we wandered Thou hast found us.
　When we doubted, sent us light;
Still Thine arm has been around us,
　All our paths were in Thy sight.

In the world will foes assail us,
　Craftier, stronger, far than we,
And the strife shall never fail us,
　Well we know before we die.
Therefore, Lord! we come believing
　Thou canst give the power we need,
Through the prayers of faith receiving
　Strength, the Spirit's strength indeed.

We would trust in Thy protecting,
   Wholly rest upon Thine arm,
Follow wholly Thy directing,
   Thou our only guard from harm;
Keep us from our own undoing,
   Help us turn to Thee when tried;
Still our footsteps, Father! viewing,
   Keep us ever at Thy side.

11. PRAYER.
12. TRIBUTE to the memory of departed members.
13. SONG —

"For Thy mercy and Thy grace,
   Faithful through another year,
Hear our song of thankfulness,
   Father and Redeemer! hear.
In our weakness and distress
   Rock of strength; be Thou our stay;
In the pathless wilderness
   Be our true and living way.

Who of us death's awful road
   In the coming year shall tread?
With Thy rod and staff, O God!
   Comfort Thou his dying head.
Keep us faithful, keep us pure,
   Keep us evermore Thine own;
Help, oh help us to endure;
   Fit us for the promised crown."

14. READ at the midnight hour as the bells ring out the old year and ring in the new, Tennyson's Hymn for the New Year—

"Ring out, wild bells, to the wild sky,
　　The flying clouds, the frosty light
　　The year is dying in the night;
Ring out, wild bells and let him die.

Ring out the old, ring in the new,
　　Ring happy bells across the snow
　　The year is going, let him go;
Ring out the false, ring in the true.

Ring out the grief that saps the mind,
　　For those that here we see no more;
　　Ring out the feud of rich and poor
Ring in redress to all mankind.

Ring out a slowly dying cause,
　　And ancient forms of party strife
　　Ring in the noble modes of life
With sweeter manners, purer laws.

Ring out the want, the care, the sin,
　　The faithless coldness of the times,
　　Ring out, ring out my mournful rhymes,
But ring the fuller minstrel in.

Ring out false pride in place and blood,
　　The civic slander and the spite;
　　Ring in the love of truth and right;
Ring in the common love of good.

A WATCH PRAYER-MEETING. 239

  Ring out old shapes of foul disease;
   Ring out the narrowing lust of gold:
   Ring out the thousand wars of old;
  Ring in the thousand years of peace.

  Ring in the valiant man and free,
   The larger heart, the kindlier hand;
   Ring out the darkness of the land,
  Ring in the Christ that is to be."

15. THE PLEDGING of the New Year with good Resolutions.
16. SONG —
   "Thou who roll'st the year around
    Crowned with mercies large and free,
   Rich Thy gifts to us abound,
    Warm our praise shall rise to Thee.
   Kindly to our worship bow,
    While our grateful thanks we tell,
   That, sustained by Thee, we now
    Bid the parting year — farewell.

  All its numbered days are spent,
   All its busy scenes are o'er,
  All its joys forever fled,
   All its sorrows felt no more.
  Mingled with the eternal past,
   Its remembrance shall decay;
  Yet to be revived at last
   At the solemn judgment-day.

All our follies, Lord, forgive!
    Cleanse us from each guilty stain;
Let Thy grace within us live,
    That we spend not years in vain.
Then, when life's last eve shall come,
    Happy spirits, may we fly
To our everlasting home,
    To our Father's house on high!"'

17. DOXOLOGY AND BENEDICTION.

CHAPTER XXV.

Ladies' Prayer-Meeting.

INASMUCH as business men have their special seasons for prayer, there is no reason why women should not have theirs. If men, harrassed by business cares, can daily snatch a few moments in the midday for spiritual devotion and religious improvement, presumably the ladies who are freed from such anxieties, can devote at least one day each week for such a meeting. The ladies have leisure for calling and meeting in societies to foster various benevolent schemes; shall they not also find leisure and relish for meetings of social prayer and religious conference? I don't know as it would be anything out of place, if the women were to hold their daily meeting, or afternoon meeting, for the increase of grace and the promotion of godliness, just the same as men have their daily noon-day meetings. Is there not some Lanphier to inaugurate such a system?

Now I am aware that novelists, like Dickens, and humorists of our day, have turned their wit to ridicule such small societies as tend to create greater interest in matters pertaining to "Borrioboola-Gha" than their own neighborhoods, or make women more busy in the affairs of other households than those which belong to their own home circles. We occasionally see such extracts as the following going the rounds of the press :

"'Is the lady of the house in?' some one has called to inquire.

"'Certainly she isn't,' the 'henpecked' husband has responded. 'She is out. She is perennially and eternally out.'

"'Where can I see her?'

"'Why, go down to the Woman Suffrage Club Rooms; and if she is not there, go to the Society for the Prevention of Cruelty to Animals; and if she has left there, visit the hall of the Association for Alleviating the Miseries of the "Senegambians;" and if she has not finished up there, look for her at the Church Aid Society, or at the Ninth Ward Soup House, or at some of these places."

This may do very well for satire, or as an exaggeration; but it has a very slender foundation in fact. Religion does not induce neglect, nor countenance idleness in anybody. Its spirit is the exact opposite. He or she that neglects to provide for the house and the household is no better than a heathen, and has denied the faith. Christianity denounces the gathering and circulating of scandal, and such neglect of home interests as is implied in "gadding about" and the being nothing better than busybodies in the affairs of others. A daily prayer-meeting, for that matter, might be instituted and carried forward without slighting a single responsibility of the home circle; in point of fact, such a meeting would prove an incentive to greater fidelity in the performance of the entire scheme of domestic duties. A prayer-meeting is the best friend that can be found to promote sweetness, purity, fidelity and light in all the relations of home and in all the sacred duties of wife, mother, or daughter.

A ladies' weekly prayer-meeting would prove itself most beneficial and invigorating to the piety of a church if it should be carried forward on the plan of visiting all the homes of the congregation. Such a plan would tend to increase the usual number, by interesting those who are not in the habit of assembling for this purpose. It would deepen the current of godliness. It would revive the faith hope and charity of the weak-hearted and the backsliding. It would arouse the careless and indifferent. It would lead many to become inquirers in the way of religion. It would foster regularity in attendance upon all the services and upon all the ordinances of the sanctuary. It would beget a lively sympathy, and strengthen the bonds of Christian love, between household and household. Whilst the wants of the home are fully looked after and not despised, something of love and beneficence would also spring up in the heart toward the poor, the neglected, and even the far-off "Senegambians." In a word, the attendance upon meetings of prayer, and the habit of prayer itself, would adorn and sanctify the home, and make it more beautiful and dignified than all the places on the earth besides. What place more sacred on earth than a godly, Christian, praying home?

Seasons of the deepest religious interest in the church set all classes to praying, as notice the following extract from the Works of President Edwards. And it is but natural when souls realize how near heaven is to them, and how important are all its concerns, that they should converse with heaven in the only language that forms a communication between earth and heaven — prayer.

"Before the first great outpouring," he writes, "of the Spirit of God on the Christian church, which began at Jerusalem, the church of God gave themselves to incessant prayer. The inhabitants of our town — at the time of the great revival — are now divided into particular praying societies; most of the people, young and old, have voluntarily associated themselves in distinct companies for mutual assistance in social worship in private houses; what I intend, therefore, is that days of prayer should be spent partly in these distinct praying companies. Such a method of keeping a fast as this has several times been proved; in the forenoon, after the duties of the family and closet, as early as might be, all the people of the congregation have gathered in their particular religious societies; companies of men by themselves, and companies of women by themselves; young men by themselves, and young women by themselves; and companies of children in all parts of the town by themselves, as many as were capable of social, religious exercises; the boys by themselves, and the girls by themselves; and about the middle of the day, at an appointed hour, all have met together in the house of God to offer up public prayers, and to hear a sermon suited to the occasion; and they have retired from the house of God again unto their private societies, and spent the remaining part of the day in praying together there." But of course seasons like these are exceptional.

A ladies' prayer-meeting to be successful, should be prompt in opening and in closing. The exercises should be short and pointed. The subject should be announced at least one week in advance. The exercises in its speaking parts should be without formality, and in a large measure, conversational. An essay might occasionally be prepared by those whose gifts lie in that direction. A poem, or other article, illustrating the subject, might be read at times to vary the exercises. A Bible reading, now and then, would prove highly edifying. There should always be much singing, and whose voice is sweeter than woman's? Let each one find out what her peculiar gift or talent may be, and then let that capacity be more fully cultivated to the edifying of all. Some may have a gift for prayer, let them pray; some for singing, let them sing; some for writing, let them write; some for reading, let them read; some for teaching, let them teach; some for exhortation, let them exhort; and some for silence, let them keep silence. There are Marthas as well as Marys. Let full freedom prevail, that so all may come for profit and delight. If there is a woman's missionary society in the church, give one meeting a month, or less often, in which to consider the spread of the Gospel in home and foreign fields, and to pray for its success. If there are other societies, let not their interests be ignored, but make them occasionally, and each in their turn, the subject of the meetings. In this way all interests will be harmonized, and workers in their peculiar spheres will sympathize more heartily with the aims and endeavors of each other, without clash or rivalry. And let it be understood that one class of work is as honorable as another, inasmuch as each and all are necessary to the well-being of Christ's kingdom. It might be well, as a last suggestion, that all the ladies in the church be divided into twelve committees, and the care and conduct of the prayer-meeting for an entire month given to each. In this way, all the gifts of the church will be called out, and more fully cultivated.

CHAPTER XXVI.

TUESDAY EVENING MEETINGS.

To Include a Training College and Other Objects.

IN many churches it is the custom to hold two regular meetings of the church, besides the Sunday services, generally on the evenings of Tuesday and Friday, the one for a prayer-meeting, and the other for a lecture, or for other purposes, both social and devotional. I suppose just as many public meetings of this kind in each week will be judicious as you can make highly profitable, interesting and inspiring. The principle to be observed is, not the number of meetings you can hold, but the kind of meetings which you can make them. It is not quantity that is to be sought after, but quality. It surely is much better to enlist your people in efforts of an improving nature, than to leave the whole week open for all sorts of recreations, amusements and worldly frivolities.

And as an example of how people respond to the labors of an earnest pastor in behalf of their spiritualities, I may give a brief transcript from the "Memoir of Dr. Edward Payson."

His church at Portland, Maine, were in the habit of keeping a quarterly day for fasting and prayer, and in this matter he had himself set a notable example by regularly observing some day in each week for fasting and secret prayer. Indeed, it is generally supposed, that the frequency with which he abstained from food for religious purposes, was a chief reason for the decline of his health and early death; and yet there can be no doubt but that these frequent fastings and his daily hours of secret prayer kept up that intense spirituality in his life which made his ministry so successful during the twenty years of his pastorate. In a letter to a young clergyman, written in 1821, Dr. Payson, to answer some questions about his pastoral labors and methods of preaching, stated that "since the failure of my health, I preach but three sermons in a week — two on the Sabbath, and one on Thursday evening. . . . I also aim to preach the truths of the Gospel in a practical and experimental, rather than a dry and speculative manner. In preaching to professing Christians, I endeavor to rouse and humble, rather than to comfort them; for, if they can be kept humble, comfort will follow, of course. Besides, I do not suppose that Christians need as much consolation now as they did in the primitive ages, when exposed to persecution.

"Our church is divided into seven districts; the

members of each district meet for prayer and conference once a month, and the brethren residing in each district are a standing committee of the church for that district, to supply the wants of the poor, and bring before the church, in due form, any case of discipline which may occur. We have a monthly meeting of all the brethren for business, a church conference every Tuesday evening, a prayer-meeting on Friday evening, a monthly prayer-meeting for the Sabbath-schools, and the monthly union concert for prayer. We have also an inquiry-meeting for males on Sabbath evening, and for females on Friday afternoon."

As the result of such multiplied work he was never without serious inquirers about the way of salvation — sometimes as high as sixty persons coming together at the same time for this purpose — and still farther, his church kept growing steadily by the accession of membership by conversion, ranging from thirty to fifty persons a year.

There is scarcely any limit to the different kinds of meetings that may be held, or as to the variety of objects that may be especially contemplated by them. What these shall be will depend upon the pastor, and the hearty co-operation of his people. A plan for a continuous series of Tuesday evening meetings, in connection with the weekly prayer-meeting on Friday evenings, to embrace a training college and other objects, has been kindly sent me by Dr. Arthur T. Pierson, pastor of the Fort Street Presbyterian Church, Detroit, Mich. The schedule is printed in full, that it may serve as a suggestion to pastors who are engaged in labors of a similar nature. I do not know, but I suppose that each member of the congregation is supplied with a copy of these subjects for use and reference:

1878.

NOVEMBER.

5. Quarterly Meeting. Christian Union. *E. Jay Carrington.*
12. Training College. "The Laws of Evidence." *Pastor.*
19. Believing on Testimony. John xx: 24–31. *Emory Wendall.*
26. Conference. Mission Work; fields and methods.
C. G. Brownell.

DECEMBER.

3. Work for Willing Hands. Nehemiah iv: 6.
Elisha A. Fraser.
10. Bible Reading. Preparation for Work. *John Cameron.*
17. Quarterly Meeting. Foreign Mission Societies. *President.*
24. Social Meeting. Dickens' Christmas Carol. *C. Buncher.*
31. The Old Year and the New. Psalm lxv. *James J. Cone.*

1879.

JANUARY.

7. The Character of Caleb. Joshua xiv: 6–15. *Bradford Smith.*
14. Training College. "The Search after Truth." I.
Rev. F. T. Bayley.

21. Training College. "The Search after Truth." II.
Rev. F. T. Bayley.
28. Training College. "The Search after Truth." III.
Rev. F. T. Bayley.

FEBRUARY.

4. Conference. How shall we find our Work. *Geo. S. Adams.*
11. Anniversary Christian Union. *E. Jay Carrington.*
18. Social Meeting. "A Trip to the Golden Gate." *Pastor.*
25. Conference. How shall we Save Young Men.
C. P. Woodruff.

MARCH.

4. Joseph's Prosperity. Genesis xxxix : 1-6. *Lucien A. Smith.*
11. Training College. The Argument for Prophecy. *Pastor.*
18. Social Meeting. Hints on the Reading of Books.
Charles Buncher.
25. God's Chosen Workers. 1 Cor. i : 26-31. *F. Hyatt Smith.*

APRIL.

1. Annual Meeting. Young Men's Foreign Miss. Society.
Charles Buncher.
8. Bible Reading. "The Sin of Neglect." *Frank G. Smith.*
15. Social Meeting. "The Paradise of the Pacific." *Pastor.*
22. The Bible a Practical Guide. Psalm cxix : 9-16.
Geo. W. Hoffman.
29. Conference. Sabbath-school Teaching. *Jos. W. Smith.*

MAY,

6. Quarterly Meeting. Christian Union. *President.*
13. Training College. "Prophecy and History." *Pastor.*
20. Called in Youth to Serve God. Jere. i : 6-9. *Geo. N. Ladue.*
27. Isaiah's Holy Zeal. Isaiah lxii : 1-7. *Theoph. Hoskins.*

JUNE.

3. Conference. How Shall We Reach the Masses?
   Wm. H. Beresford.
10. Bible Reading. Overcoming Temptation. *A. G. Hibbard.*
17. Social Meeting. "A Talk on Shells." *Bry. Walker.*
24. Praise Meeting. David's Psalms. *F. Lambie.*

JULY.

1. Quarterly Meeting Foreign Missionary Societies. *President.*
   (Papers on Ignatius Loyola and Fidelia Fiske.)
8. Learning by Teaching. Isaiah 1: 4. *A. P. Sherrill.*
15. Holy Living and Prayer. Matt. vi : 5–7. *E. O. Windsor.*
22. Holy Living and Giving. Matt. vi : 1–5. *Jno. Bristow.*
29. Doing What We Can. Mark xiv : 1–9. *W. A. Whittlesey.*

AUGUST.

5. Quarterly Meeting. Christian Union. *President.*
12. Bible Reading. The Power of Prayer. *J. R. Dutton.*
19. Social Meeting. "A Talk on Health." *D. Inglis, M. D.*
26. Christ Our Example. I. Peter ii : 21–25. *G. H. Earle.*

SEPTEMBER.

2. Sanctified Vessels. II. Tim. ii : 19–21. *H. M. Parke.*
9. Conference. Duties of Church Members. *E. C. Walker.*
16. Training College. Argument from Miracles I. *Pastor.*
23. Conference. "Serving the Lord in Business." *S. P. Wilcox.*
30. Praise Meeting. Hymns of the Ages. *F. Lambie.*

OCTOBER.

7. For. Missionary Societies. Semi-annual. "Japan."
   President.

14. Bible Reading. "The Holy Young Men of Scripture."
J. B. Irvine, jr.
21. Social Meeting. "The Service of Sacred Song." *Pastor.*
28. Conference. Directing Inquirers to Christ. *Jno. Cameron.*

NOVEMBER.

4. Quarterly Meeting. Christian Union. *President.*
11. Conference. "Young Mens' Christian Association."
W. McMillan.
18. Training College. Argument from Miracles II. *Pastor.*
25. Promise Meeting. "The Heavenly Inheritance."
A. T. Henderson.

DECEMBER.

2. Lost Opportunities. Matthew xxv. *W. Buhl.*
9. Bible Reading. "Responsibility to God." *M. C. Huyett.*
16. Social Meeting. "Longfellow and his Poems." *C. Buncher.*
23. Life and Death. II. Cor. iv: 16: to v. 9. *Douglas Payne.*
30. Quarterly Meeting. For. Miss'n Societies. *President.*
    (Papers on Alex. Duff and Harriet Newell.)

CHAPTER XXVII.

YOUNG MEN'S SATURDAY NIGHT PRAYER-MEETINGS.

THESE meetings, in their nature and methods, do not differ from other meetings for prayer. Their object, apart from the spiritual good they are calculated to do, is, as I suppose, to enable young men among themselves to pray and speak with a greater sense of freedom, and prepare them for active co-operation in the weekly church prayer-meeting. In many churches a young peoples' meeting is held on Sabbath evening just before the public services. In the Fourteenth street Presbyterian Church, New York city, Rev. F. H. Marling, pastor, a prayer-meeting is held every Saturday evening, for half an hour, exclusively for young men, which has proved itself very successful and efficient. By the following schedule it will be seen that their work is laid out very systematically from one summer's vacation to another. How profitable it must be for young men thus actively to engage in their own spiritual improvement—the culture of their gifts and graces—and to throw a good influence around their comrades—"come thou with us and we will do thee good"—amid the many temptations of city life, I need not stop to enlarge upon! Nor do I introduce their list of subjects with names of their leaders, because I suppose that every church can enter into just the same kind of work; they may not have the young men, or they may be carrying on all the public meetings that it is judicious for a church to prosecute—let every thing be done thoroughly; but I do give it so that, where circumstances are similar, and a field for this kind of labor is opened, the field may be worked, and useful hints gathered from their experience. I remember that a writer in kindly reviewing "The Prayer-Meeting And Its Improvement," said that, "It is not likely that any one would undertake to carry out all the suggestions of this author; for no two could be found with notions so exactly alike that these details would equally please them. . . . But methods might be selected from this book that would greatly assist leaders, both clerical and lay."

I agree with him fully, but I must not have said it as clearly as it ought to have been said in that book; but now, lest it be said against this book, that it designs to establish a church with a continuous session of various forms of prayer-meetings, I hasten to deny such intention. Each church may have a field of labor peculiar to itself; let that peculiarity be fully met and fully developed. Train it into a glorious success for the Master.

In one, it may be an auxiliary cottage prayer-meeting; in another, a woman's meeting; in a third, an Aaron and Hur Society, and in a fourth, something else. Do not undertake too much, but do well what you undertake, and if in these pages of hints, gathered from many sources, you find anything to help you, give God the praise.

1878-79.

OCTOBER.

5. Reunion, One in Christ. John 17 : 6-21. Leader, *F. A. Ferris.*
12. Subject, "Young Man Arise." Luke 7 : 11-16.
A. C. Donaldson.
19. Subject, "Fear Not." Isa. 41 : 10; 43 : 1. Matt. 10 : 28.
C. B. Sanders.
26. Subject, "Stand Fast." I. Cor. 16 : 13. Phil. 1 : 27-30.
A. E. Marling.

NOVEMBER.

2. Subject, "Be Strong." Psa. 27 : 13, 14. Eph. 6 : 10-18.
John H. Jewett.
9. Subject, "Take Heed." Josh. 22 : 5. Luke 12 : 15. Rev. 22 : 19.
Geo. U. Dixon.
16. Subject, "Put Away Evil." Eccl. 11 : 9, 10. II. Tim. 2 : 22.
A. F. Denniston.
23. Subject, "Be Thankful." Psa. 103 : 1-5. Col. 3 : 15-17.
F. H. O. Marling.
30. Subject, "Wrong Places." Gen. 19 : 15-26. Prov. 4 : 14, 15.
R. F. Denniston.

DECEMBER.

7. Subject, "Our Right Place," Luke 24 : 49. Mark 8 : 34–38.
Psa. 16 : 5–11. *M. A. White.*
14. Subject, "Peace Our Portion." John 14 : 27. Isa. 26 : 3, 4.
Wm. H. Curtis.
21. Subject, "Christmas Tidings." Isa. 9 : 6, 7. *C. E. Marling.*
28. Subject, "The Old Year's Lessons." Psa. 90 : 3–17.
W. E. McNeille.

JANUARY.

4. Subject, "The New Year's Promise." Luke 12 : 32. Isa. 55 : 8–13. *H. H. Uhler.*
11. Subject, "Casting Our Lot." Heb. 11 : 24–27. Deut. 34 : 10–12. *W. B. Haulenbeek.*
18. Subject, "Our Defence." Psa. 5 : 11, 12. Psa. 31 : 1–3.
W. A. Cape.
25. Subject, "Our Prayers." Matt. 6 : 5–15. *A. T. Prentice.*

FEBRUARY.

1. Subject, "A Wise Choice." I. Kings 3 : 5–14. *M. L. Stewart.*
8. Subject, "A Foolish Choice." Mark 10 : 17–22.
M. P. Welcher.
15. Subject, "Peril of Choosing Wrong." Prov. 1 : 24–33.
Geo. L. Hubbell.
22. Subject, "Our Power for Good." Prov. 20 : 29. Eph 6 : 10–18.
W. P. Uhler.

MARCH.

1. Subject, "Our Power for Evil." I. Kings 11 : 28 ; 12 : 26–30.
Eccl. 9 : 18. *C. J. Haulenbeek.*
8. Subject, "Genuine Faith." Matt. 13 : 44–52. *F. H. Wisewell.*

15. Subject, "Far-reaching Faith." Matt. 9: 20–30.   *C. Burchard.*
22. Subject, "Practical Faith." Jas. 1: 22–27.   *C. E. Fladd.*
29. Subject, "A Personal Saviour." John 8: 12–28.   *H. H. Uhler.*

APRIL.

5. Subject, "Our Eye Single." Matt. 6: 9–23. Deut. 5: 32.
W. M. Lewis.
12. Subject, "Two Conditions Contrasted." Luke 15: 11–32.
W. Ord.
19. Subject, "The Great Difference." Isa. 33: 13–17. Deut. 32: 29–33.   *A. E. Marling.*
26. Subject, "Indulging Self." Luke 14: 16–24. Haggai 1: 4–10.
J. Heath.

MAY.

3. Subject, "Covenant Obligations." Eccl. 5: 1–5. Rom. 6: 1–5.
W. E. McNeille.
10. Subject, "Being Satisfied with Truth." II. Tim. 4: 1–8.
A. F. Denniston.
17. Subject, "Prophesying Evil." Num. 14: 26–29.
F. H. O. Marling.
24. Subject, "Growth in Grace." II. Pet. 3: 18. Mark 4: 26–32.
A. C. Donaldson.
31. Subject, "Vacation Counsel." Gen. 45: 24. Jude 21–25.
F. A. Ferris.

CHAPTER XXVIII.

Sunday Morning Meetings for Prayer.

I HAD better put myself square on the record once more, inasmuch as so many different kinds of prayer-conferences, and times of holding them, find a description in this book and say that I do not seriously propose that any single church shall undertake all of them, nor follow all the suggestions of this book, nor of the one that preceded it. But what I do mean is this, that where circumstances are similar, such meetings as are here described can be held to profit on the part of others, by following the methods which in these cases have made them successful.

If your church is a praying church, like Gen. Havelock it will seek out places for holding meetings, rather than to get along with a minimum amount of praying, and with but one meeting a week.

Havelock was a lieutenant in the army that captured Rangoon, the capital of Burmah, and set free the English captives that had been kept as prisoners within it. He was then a praying lieutenant, as he afterwards was a praying general, and the city was no sooner in the power of the English than he set out to find a place that might be used for holding a prayer-meeting. Where do you think he found one?

"There was a famous heathen temple in a retired grove," we are told, "which was devoted to the service of Buddha. He secured one of the chambers in it, a large room filled with images of the gods, sitting all around, with their legs crossed, and arms folded on their laps. One day as an officer was strolling round the temple, he thought he heard the sound of English singing; he stopped and hearkened. A strange sound here he thought; but it certainly was the sound of psalm-singing, in good old English style. What did it mean — how accounted for? He determined to follow the sound, and behold, it led him to an upper chamber, where Havelock, with his Bible and hymn-book before him, surrounded by more than a hundred of his soldiers, was holding a prayer-meeting. The room was dark, but every idol had a lamp in his lap, shedding more light than any idols had ever done before. Did he read do you think, the 115th Psalm for their Scripture lesson?"

I desire, then, to intimate, as clearly as I can, that each church should make such a selection of meetings, as to number, times, means and methods, as shall make **each and all successful as to attendance and spiritual** good. I am convinced, also, that just what may prove successful with one church, will not with another, and therefore such a large number of actual meetings have been inserted in these pages, that they may serve as hints to the discovery by each church of its largest measure of spiritual usefulness.

A Sabbath morning prayer-meeting is held in some churches to acknowledged good on the part of those who attend.

"I have been endeavoring," writes Dr. Payson, "to establish among us what are called Aaron and Hur Societies, i. e., little collections of four or five or more persons, who meet before service on Sabbath morning, to spend an hour in prayer for a blessing on the minister and the ordinances. They began on New Year's Day, and we seemed to have immediate answer, for the meeting was unusually solemn; and we have reason to hope that the Word was not preached in vain."

These Aaron and Hur Societies, to which reference is made, formed an important feature in the New England revival of 1799.

" The flame (of revival) at once caught," wrote Judge Boudinot, to Judge Reeve, in giving a sketch of them, "the hearts of the truly pious among us. The next Sabbath morning a number agreed to form a society to meet at nine o'clock, and spend an hour previous to going to church in prayer to God for his blessing on the Word. They styled themselves the Aaron and Hur Society, as supporting the hands of their minister. It was not long before the blessed work pervaded every part of the congregation."

Knowing that a meeting of this class was kept up by the Second Presbyterian Church of Indianapolis, I addressed a note to Dea. O. K. Coe for a brief history of it, and received in reply the following succinct statement :

"In regard to our Sabbath morning meeting, I would say," he writes, "it started some twenty-five years ago when Henry Ward Beecher was pastor, by a few members of the church coming in at nine o'clock in the morning and spending an hour in praying, singing, and in social converse. It has been kept up without interruption since then. Quite a number of its original members have died, but others have come in to fill their places. All who attend this meeting love it and prize it as a valuable spiritual help. The manner of conducting it has been quite different from time to time. Six years ago, when I joined it, the plan was to have a leader who started some subject to talk and pray about, and at the close he would appoint some one to take charge of the next meeting, and so on; but, lately, we have dropped that plan, and we now take the subject on our printed topic list for the next Thursday evening meeting. We read the chapter from which the verse is taken in the topic list, and then use perfect freedom in talking on the subject, and thereby get many useful hints for the coming week-day prayer-meeting of the church. We have all found it an excellent help in starting us right for the Sabbath services, in preparing the heart for hearing, and in looking for immediate spiritual blessing. It proves itself thus, in the experience of us all, to be one of the most profitable meetings of the week."

What a great help to the preacher such a praying band as this must prove! He cannot but feel that he is preaching in a warm and loving spiritual atmosphere, and that the field is made ready for the sowing of the seed. Let us suppose that the pastor, likewise, has prepared himself for the preaching, as these have for hearing, by a season of close communion with God in prayer, and will he not, like Whitefield on similar occasions, go from the study and the closet to the pulpit and the people "as if there was a rainbow about his head?"

"And Moses said unto Joshua, choose us out men and go out to fight with Amalek: to-morrow I will stand on the top of the hill with the rod of God in my hand. So Joshua did as Moses had said to him, and fought with Amalek: and Moses, Aaron, and Hur went up to the top of the hill. And it came to pass, when Moses held up his hand that Israel prevailed; and when he let down his hand, Amalek prevailed. But Moses' hands were heavy; and they took a stone, and put it under him, and he sat thereon: and Aaron and Hur stayed up his hands, the one on the one side, and the other on the other side: and his hands were steady until the going down of the sun."

CHAPTER XXIX.

Children's Inquiry and Prayer-Meeting.

IT has been a complaint that by far too little attention has been given by pastors to special religious services for children. "No longer ago than 1855," remarks Rev. H. Clay Trumbull, "in the preface to a collection of sermons to youth chiefly from English ministers, published by Carlton and Porter, under the title of 'The Child's Preacher,' the editor remarked, in explanation cf the fact that but little of the material was supplied by American ministers, 'that we have not similar contributions from other American preachers is not because we have failed to solicit them. The truth is that American ministers have as yet written but few sermons to children; and, indeed, have preached quite too few.' Even at the present time it is not uncommon for a pastor to refer to his inability to preach fittingly to children, as though it were after all a matter of no serious moment. 'I confess I cannot preach to children,' or 'I have no tact in that line' is uttered much as would be the statement 'I have never studied Italian,' or 'I have no special fondness for chemistry, or mechanics.' Says the Rev. H. C. McCook, in the S. S. *Times*, 'I once asked a reverend doctor of divinity, who was present in my Sunday-School, to talk to the children. "I never talk to children!" That was the answer, with an expressive shake of the head, and a matter-of-surprise-and-of-course sort of tone, that sent me away humble and sorry for my offending. I felt as though I ought to apologize! Is not such a treatment of this matter more common than excusable?'"

There are at present some very successful preachers to children, such as Dr. Tyng, Dr. Newton, Rev. E. P. Hammond, and Rev. E. M. Long, who have preached regularly to children, either once each Sabbath, or once each month, and though their numbers are increasing, it is still by no means a regular custom in all our churches. I am convinced that the cause of religion suffers from this neglect of the children. As pastors we should seek and labor and pray for their early and immediate conversion. Dr. Spencer, whose pastorate was very successful, made it a rule to especially look after the religious interests of the young and of the old above sixty, and he attributed much of his success to that principle of pastoral work.

Many valuable suggestions for work among children will be found in Mr. Trumbull's book on "The Children in the Temple." After having described a variety of children's services, he takes up the heading of our chapter and goes on to say, "that some of the most successful workers among children, seldom or never preach without holding an inquiry-meeting at the close of the service — a meeting at which the children may be separately addressed and counselled by intelligent followers of Christ.

"The prominence which efforts of this character have obtained, indicates the readiness of the church to avail itself of such an agency. God has seemingly prepared the way by his Spirit and providence for this mode of working to bring little ones into his fold. There has been a felt want of personal contact of the preacher with the soul preached to. Says Dr. Duryea, in pressing the advantages enjoyed by the Sunday-school teacher, 'while the minister is teaching all about the Gospel, here is a soul that wants a direct application of the Gospel. The religious teaching from the pulpit is not sufficient. There must be a special teaching mouth to ear, mind to mind, heart to heart. Just as a student of medicine may want to lecture on medicine, but a sick man knowing his sickness, wants a prescription, so the Christian student may want a lecture on religion, but he wants again and again a prescription, for his soul.' And while the minister has thus prized the privileges of the class-teacher, that teacher has not been without a longing for yet other advantages in his efforts to win the young to Jesus.

"'Many a zealous Sunday-school teacher,' says an English worker, on Mr. Hammond's plan, 'has doubtless often felt the need of something supplimentary to the ordinary class-teaching and school services — something calculated to give every scholar a medium of sympathy and heart contact with his teacher. He has felt sure that there were some dear scholars in his class who were secret disciples of the Lord Jesus, and others whose minds were evidently impressed with Divine truth; and often has he longed for some kind of magnet, so to speak, which would irresistibly draw forth from the anxious a candid confession of their state of mind. There is about our present Sunday-school system an amount of, perhaps necessary, order and formality, which prevents him from seeing the fruit of his labors and fails to give him an opportunity of eliciting what impressions have been made on the minds of his scholars.' He there argues in favor of the childrens' meetings instituted by Mr. Hammond, and adduces reasons for believing 'that in these children's services and inquiry-meetings, is to be found the long missing link.' And the meetings thus commended are more fully described, as follows:

"'The services are held in the school-room of Surrey

Chapel (Newman Hall's), on Sunday evening, at half-past six, and on Tuesday evening at seven. On Sunday the attendance averages about three hundred, and would be larger if all applicants were admitted. On Tuesday there are generally from one hundred to one hundred and fifty. In conducting these meetings the aim has been to make them as varied and interesting as possible, and to bring all the exercises down to the capacity of the children. The prayers and addresses are exceedingly short and simple. There is plenty of singing and the tunes are lively, many of the hymns having a chorus.

"'But the characteristic feature of the services, and the one which we think has been most productive of good, is that which is called, for want, I think, of a better name, the inquiry-meeting. At the close of the preliminary meeting an invitation is given to the children who love Jesus, and those who want to love Jesus, to remain behind that the teachers may talk to them and pray with them. About half — or sometimes two-thirds — will stop, and the rest leave while a hymn is being sung. The teachers and friends present, then gather classes around them, and, without taking any formal lesson or subject, speak to the children simply and earnestly about heavenly things, and strive to impress on them individually, and personally, the duty of giving their hearts to the Saviour. There is not much order or arrangement about these classes — teachers speak to the children nearest them, or to any they may see — but those who come regularly often get the same children from week to week.' "

" The most satisfactory results are reported from similar meetings in other parts of Great Britain, and like services have been richly blessed in various portions of this country. Such an agency, coming thus approved, should not be lightly passed by, by those desiring the greatest good of the children.

" House, and Pardee, and other American writers, on Sunday-school themes, commend warmly regular prayer-meetings for the children, and many pastors and superintendents make much of them. 'Some of our Sunday-schools,' says Pardee, ' hold such a meeting at the close of each afternoon session.' The boys and the girls being in separate rooms, under leaders of their own sex, respectively, 'the meeting opens with singing a familiar hymn, and then a few appropriate verses and remarks just adapted to kindle devotion in the little hearts, and then the little prayers follow freely and almost spontaneously. They soon learn to love to pray, and pray in real faith too, for the whole life of a little child is a life of faith.' "

" In some churches at the West, an organization

known as 'The Faithful Band,' gathers young believers for culture in the Christian life. This resembles the Methodist class-meeting in its main features, and serves as a training school for youthful disciples, directing them to active effort for other souls, while aiding them in the cultivation of grace in their own renewed hearts.

"Thus, in various ways, the children are finding their proper place in the temple, and their part in its services. Through Bible study and recitation, in prayer and praise, as listeners to the preached word and to its application to their individual consciences, as helpers of each other in the divine life, and as workers together with each other with Jesus, they are being won to the Redeemer and upreared in his service. So are being answered the prayer of the Psalmist, and of so many who have come after him, 'That our sons may be as plants grown up in their youth; that our daughters may be as corner-stones, polished after the similitude of a palace.'"

CHAPTER XXX.

Cottage Prayer-Meetings.

And How To Conduct Them.

SOCIAL meetings of this kind are known by various names, such as cottage, or neighborhood prayer-meetings. Their especial object is to visit those who never or rarely attend the social meetings of the church. Besides the unconverted, there are aged and sick persons, who do not attend these mid-week gatherings. Their field then is to induce neglecters of public worship to become regular attendants, to institute meetings in places of destitution and neglect (such as the tenement houses), and to bring the means of grace to those, who by reason of infirmity, are kept at home. It might, therefore, be a good plan for each church during the winter months, when life is necessarily more within doors, to hold weekly or bi-weekly meetings on Friday evenings, if the way be clear, at the homes of the membership, to be led by competent persons, with or without the attendance of the pastor, as may be deemed most convenient. I am sure such a practice as this would tend to elevate the spiritual life of the church, as well as greatly sanctify the homes of your membership. It would draw your people nearer together and intensify their religious experience and communion. Try it.

For the following wise suggestions on methods and objects for the ordinary meetings of this class, I am indebted to Mr. C. H. Whiting, formerly of Burlington, Iowa, and now secretary of railroad work at Detroit, Mich.:

" The importance of this branch of our work cannot be overestimated. Especially after having left us the noble example of the Apostles in the early church (Acts v. 42) 'And in every house they ceased not to teach and preach Jesus Christ.' Also we have the command of the Great Teacher (Mark xvi. 15) 'Go ye into all the world, and preach the gospel to every creature.' The work is important, then, because thus *commanded*. And although in most places in our land, we have churches sufficiently large to accommodate almost the entire population, still many, I might say the majority, are, from growing habits from childhood of indifference, or prejudice against them, seldom if ever found within the sacred walls of God's house. The work is important, then, because many would perhaps never hear the 'glad tidings of great joy,' without this means of grace. It is also important, because it develops Christian workers, and stimulates them. There are many young men, Christians, whose hearts are burning with love to their Saviour, and who yearn to do something for Him, but who do not feel capable of undertaking many of the kinds of Christian work by which they are surrounded: who, by attending these meetings, are led, ere long, to speak a word for Christ, and before hardly aware of it, are doing the Master's will, and developing into earnest, zealous Christian workers.

"It is also important because it incites families to read and study God's Word, with whom heretofore it has been almost entirely neglected. The children, too, who are frequently in attendance at these meetings, are also interested in Bible study and are brought into the Sabbath-schools, as not unfrequently mission Sabbath-schools are started out of neighborhoods where meetings have been held.

"*How to Start a Cottage-Meeting.*

"There being in this, as in all kinds of Christian work, discouragements, those undertaking it should fully appreciate, and have implicit faith in the precious promises given us in the Word of God, and should seek importunately, that best of gifts, which our heavenly

Father is so ready to bestow upon us, viz: the gift of the Holy Spirit.

"In starting a cottage-meeting, the aim should be to take the blessed Gospel of Christ into the neglected portions of our towns and cities; into families that seldom if ever attend any of the stated means of grace. To accomplish this, those that enter upon this work should take a district in which they desire to work, visiting each house, ascertaining from the several families whether they would like a meeting at their houses or not; at same time asking if there should be a meeting held in the neighborhood, if they would attend; telling them the singing would be good, and that the meetings are being carried on by no particular denomination, by the Young Mens' Christian Association (as in some cases were you to go from a particular church, admittance would not be gained). In some instances definite answers cannot be given at once. Then give time for advisement, telling them you would call again. And call after reasonable time. When once admittance is gained into a house, ask the persons at whose house the meeting is held, to invite all their neighbors and friends. At same time it would be well to visit those families already visited, telling them of the meeting; where it would be and when, urging them to attend. Appoint the meeting at a house when it will be convenient for all house-keepers in the vicinity to attend. Then commence the meeting promptly on time, as always by negligence in commencing a meeting (if once done) persons are likely to think 'well it isn't of much importance whether I am at the meeting at the exact time or not, as they seldom ever commence on time.' At least two that can take part should make it a point to be present at each meeting, and one should be able to conduct the singing.

"*How To Conduct Them?*

"In conducting these meetings *all* stereotyped methods or plans should be discarded, varying the services as much as possible. Make the singing a prominent feature, having the hymns selected before the meeting, so that everything may move along in orderly manner. Never read a Scripture lesson so long, that the children present will become restless. Nor so low, or so fast, that the eldest cannot hear distinctly what is read. Let the Gospel truths be briefly but very plainly stated, and the plan of salvation made so plain that the children may understand it. Bible readings are very profitably used. But in new districts it is often difficult to get the persons attending to take part, as many will be found (among the ladies and elderly persons) who are not in the habit of reading or speaking; so that when Bible readings are used the leader or leaders should have the passages so marked in their own Bibles, as to be able to turn readily to them. After having held meetings some time in a district where nearly all have learned the tunes sufficiently well to take a lively part in them, a praise and prayer-meeting can be advantageously used. Setting before them the thanksgiving and praise that is comely — Heb. 13. 15 — ' By Him therefore let us offer the sacrifice of praise to God continually: that is the fruit of our lips giving thanks to His name.' Encouraging those present to take part by repeating some verse of Scripture bearing on the subject; by remarks, or by request for prayer, aim to make the services pleasant, cheerful and informal as possible.

"Do not be discouraged if only two or three are gathered together, you have enough to claim '*the promise.*' Large meetings are not essential to success. Close the meeting within the hour. If it has been very interesting so much the better. Close it and keep up the interest. After which try and secure a few words of personal conversation with those present. Especially those who appear to be interested.

"*How to Maintain Them*

"Never disappoint the people by failure to be present at the appointed time; no matter what the weather is, let it be understood you will be on hand. Nothing will so quickly or effectually kill a meeting, as to let it go by default. As before stated, have the time of commencing, understood by all. The leader should be present at least five minutes before time, to open it. It is a good plan to have printed or written invitations, and distribute them either on the day of the meeting or afterwards, to those present to give out, for the week following; and through them reach the neighborhood. Visit those especially interested during the week. Also any who may be sick among them. Religious newspapers and tracts being distributed at the close of the meetings. Illustrated Sunday-school papers to the children are the means of great good; and interest many in the meetings, as they feel you have some interest in them. After the meeting, before leaving the house, try and make the acquaintance of those present by shaking hands with them, as they pass out; thanking them for their presence and good attention and asking them to come again, as often, on account of backwardness, and a lack of cordiality on the part of those at whose house the meeting is held, some feel awkward and strange, and are not likely to return again."

CHAPTER XXXI.

The Family Meeting for Worship.

THE practice of morning and evening prayer in the family, is a general custom in the households of evangelical Christians. No one ought to consider his piety of an active stamp who neglects to institute the church in his house.

First, it is a duty. The casual reader of the Scriptures will be surprised to learn that the Bible nowhere directly commands family worship. Is it therefore an act of supererogation? Not at all. It is a duty by inference. When Abraham moved his tent to the plain of Mamre, he built there also an altar unto the Lord — Gen. 13: 18. This was an altar for family worship nigh his tent. The truly pious take their religion and its active duties with them wherever they dwell or sojourn. When David says, "Seven times a day do I praise Thee," we are to remember in explaining its meaning that during his day there was no temple in Jerusalem, and that at least two of these seven times may refer to morning and evening worship at the family altar.

Matthew Henry remarks upon Dan. 6: 10, that the beloved prophet "prayed in his house, sometimes himself alone, and sometimes with his family about him;" and on Acts 10: 30, that Cornelius likewise was a man that prayed in his house. "Every house not only may be, but ought to be, a house of prayer; where we have a tent God must have an altar, and on it we must offer spiritual sacrifices."

Paul has highly honored his faithful friends, Priscilla and Aquila, by twice writing about the church that was in their house. Rom. 16: 3, and I. Cor. 16: 19. What a beautiful compliment is paid to their worth by this designation. Some have beautifully interpreted this to refer to family worship — "their home was a sanctuary and their family a church." I would not insist upon this as its full and exclusive meaning; but if others, and among them, the early Christians, were in the habit of meeting in some family for worship, may we not believe that the family itself met for worship?

At all events, we may claim that family prayer conforms to the command, and is entitled to the promise of James 4: 8, "Draw nigh to God and He will draw nigh to you." We may also infer that it is a duty by example. It can hardly be doubted that the deeply pious in all times have prayed with and for their families in their households.

"Abraham, Joshua, David, Job, Daniel," says Matthew Henry, "all worshipped God in the family, and our Saviour confirmed the obligation; for He often prayed with His disciples as His family or household."

Secondly, it is a privilege. Family prayer binds the household more closely and lovingly together. It is a great boon to consecrate the day with prayer, before the household separates on its divers ways, and on its manifold duties. What if they should never all meet again? To have omitted it on such a day — the day of accident and separation — would prove a lasting regret. How precious at night, ere kindly sleep enwraps us all with its mantle, to commit our souls and bodies to that Guardian of Israel who neither slumbers nor sleeps, as well as to render thanks for the mercies and special providences of the closing day, for its opportunities to do good, and supplicate the divine forgiveness upon all its transgressions. This gives a gracious opportunity to pray with our children and for our children.

"Family worship," observes the sainted Cecil, "may be used as an engine of vast power in a family. It diffuses a sympathy through the members. It calls the mind off from the deadening effects of worldly affairs. It arrests every member with a morning and evening sermon, in the midst of all the hurries and cares of life. It says, 'There is a God!' 'There is a spiritual world!' 'There is a life to come!' It fixes the idea of responsibility in the mind. It furnishes a tender and judicious father or master with an opportunity of gently glancing at faults, where a direct admonition might be inexpedient. It enables him to relieve the weight with which subordination or service sits on minds of inferiors."

Dr. C. L. Thompson, editor of *The Interior* and pastor of the Third Church, Pittsburgh, has given some very pertinent hints in an article on "Family Worship," which it gives me pleasure to transcribe and incorporate with this chapter. He first describes two ways in which it is common to conduct — either with undue haste or tedious length — and then goes on to outline a happy medium:

"If it is morning," he says, "there is plenty of time, for it; if in the evening, it is right after supper, before the sleepy time. If there is a piano in the house, one of the daughters takes her place there, a little one distributes the books. There is an air of animation in the household as if something pleasant were going to be done. A hymn is given out. It is not 'China' or 'Hamburg.' It is something with life in its movement as well as religion in its words. Every voice joins. Even the baby has caught the sounds, and sings, if not correctly, at least heartily. True, she sometimes makes a comical mistake in the words. The other evening she misinterpreted 'stranded wreck' and after the manner of the world sang lustily, 'Leave the poor old strangled wretch and pull for the shore.' Then the children laughed. No matter. There was no irreverence there, and the song went piously on. The singing over, each one opens his Bible, and the reading is either responsive or around the circle, from the oldest to the youngest. Sometimes there is no reading at all, but a recitation in concert, or the offering of a verse from memory by each in turn.

"'Then — that a collection being learned at it, may not be regarded as an impertinence at church — the baby passes a little box to receive the pennies that are eagerly saved for this benevolent fund. The prayer that follows is not stereotyped. It is made up out of daily experiences and wants. It touches every family interest. It is pláin to the little child. It impresses all with the idea that God is the God of the house, and that his service is a joy and not a burden.

And, then, perhaps it closes with the Lord's Prayer, repeated in concert — not hurriedly nor pompously, but the joint loving appeal of the family to the 'Father in Heaven.' And children who look back from the toil of after years to such a family altar, see it shining with countless sustaining influences, and wreathed with tender and deathless memories." Sure enough.

In some denominations there are certain standards of faith which parents are anxious their children should learn. A question in the catechism might be committed to memory each day, and repeated at family worship the next morning, either unitedly or separately, and then a few remarks might be made to illustrate its meaning for the benefit of the children. It would take less than a year to go through the catechism in this way, and thoroughly entrust its contents to the memory.

I have been informed that it was a custom in the family of Gov. Hendrick's father to ask, and answer in rotation, questions from the Westminster Shorter Catechism. For instance, the father would ask the person sitting next to him on the right :

"What is the chief end of man?"

The answer being correctly given, the one who gave it would immediately ask the one next to him :

"What rule hath God given to direct us how we may glorify and enjoy him?"

In this way they would go round the circle, and in the course of time acquire as great a familiarity with the famous one hundred and seven questions and answers of that catechism as with the letters of the alphabet.

There is thus a great variety of methods by which to enliven the family reading and recitation at morning and evening prayers, that will fill the moments with delighful instruction, and at the same time relieve them of all monotony, repetition and tedium.

Now there may be some who, for one reason or another, cannot profitably lead the family in extempore prayer, who would find it not less a cross than a failure, to whom we would recommend the use of printed forms or studies in prayer. Entered into heartily, there is no reason why the service may not be fruitful of spiritual good. At all events the reading of prayers in the family is better than no prayers at all. Any bookseller can furnish the applicant with excellent books of this kind, such as Jay's "Morning" and "Evening" Exercises, so that no one, whatever his gifts, need omit this delightful service.

Are you a prayerless Christian? Do you pray in

THE FAMILY MEETING FOR WORSHIP.

secret? Do you keep the fires burning brightly and continually upon the family altar? Do you excuse yourself because of non-ability, or lack of confidence? Do you make the family meeting for worship cheerful with song, instructive with Scripture, hallowed with prayer, and precious in all its memories?

CHAPTER XXXII.

THE FULTON STREET NOONDAY PRAYER-MEETING.

WE have already referred to the origin of this meeting. Some very interesting particulars connected with its organization and work were elicited in an interview which the Rev. J. K. Funk* had with Mr. Lanphier, one of its founders.

"My early education," said Mr. Lanphier, "was neglected. I learned the tailor trade in Albany. Afterward I started business in this city. I was not a Christian, but was a strict moral man. Finally, I was made to see that I was a sinner and needed to be born again. One day, at the hour of noon, I found peace by believing in Christ.

"Ever after, the hour of noon was sacred. It was to me a sweet hour of prayer. In 1857, an elder of this

---

* Rev. Mr. Funk is the editor of *The Preacher and Homeletic Monthly*, New York, and deserves the thanks of the public for being the first to open his journal to a regular department for prayer-meeting services. It is to be hoped that his conspicuous example will be followed by the religious press, and that very generally we shall have attention directed to the importance of this service, and to ways and means for sustaining the interest and attendance.

church — it was known as the Old Dutch Church — persuaded me that it was my duty to be its lay missionary. I could not feel that I had qualifications for this work, my education had been so neglected; but he would not let me go. I made it a matter of prayer. Finally, I felt myself called to the work, and gave up my business, to the disgust of my partner, who pronounced me a fool. The salary given me was $800. I visited from house to house, engaged in prayer if opportunity offered, talked to business men, and invited children to the Sabath-school. Soon the work began to tell, in an increased attendance at our regular Friday evening prayer-meeting, and Sabbath services.

"The summer of '57, as you know, was a time of great business depression. I met Christian business men on the street. We talked on religion. I asked them to come in here and pray with me a few moments. During that summer, almost any hour, you could have found two or more Christians in our old meeting-room in prayer. In September of that year, I felt that it would be well to have a prayer-meeting for business men, at the hour of noon. I chose that hour, I suppose, because it was so precious an hour to me. I consulted with no one but God. I drew up the plan. It was to be a business men's meeting for prayer; to begin at the hour of noon, to last just one hour;

people to be permitted to come in and to go out at any time. There was to be no constraint. It was to be understood that coming in and going out would disturb no one, so that business men, who had but ten minutes to spare, could run in, in their shirt-sleeves for that matter, join in a single prayer and one hymn, and then go back to business. It was to be wholly informal. It was to avoid all things that were controversial, to be based on the points on which all Christians were agreed. Episcopalian and Methodist, Presbyterian and Baptist, Lutheran, all were to find this a prayer-meeting home. . . . .

"Here are the rules which we hand to the man who is to lead the meeting, for any day, to guide him:

The Usual Daily Order of Conducting the Meeting, but not Imperative.

"'Open with singing.
"'Read the Scripture.
"'Read half of the requests (at 12:30 the remainder).
"'Prayer.
"'Singing.
"'Throw the meeting open. (You have fifteen minutes of time for the above. Say, brethren, be prompt, concise, and keep within the five minutes, in order that many may take part).
"'Sing often, read one verse of each hymn you give out. If any exceed their time, manifest it by rising. Close promptly at one o'clock.
"'Benediction.'

"If a lady gets up any time during the service, you get up and ask her if it is a request she wishes to make; and you stand while she makes it, and ask some one to pray, or sing a verse of some hymn, as you please."

In order to give strangers a good understanding of the character of these meetings the following faithful report of one, as a specimen, was published in 1858, by Dr. T. W. Chambers, in his history of

The Noon Prayer-Meeting.

"We take our seat in the middle of the room," wrote he, "ten minutes before twelve o'clock, M. A few ladies are seated in one corner, and a few business men are scattered here and there through the room. Five minutes to twelve, the room begins to fill up rapidly. Two minutes to twelve, the leader passes in, and takes his seat in the desk or pulpit. At twelve M. punctual to the moment, at the first stroke of the clock, the leader rises and commences the meeting by reading two or three verses of the hymn,

"'Salvation, oh! the joyful sound,
'Tis pleasure to our ears;
A sovereign balm for every wound,
A cordial for our fears.'

"Each person finds a hymn-book in his seat; all sing with heart and voice. The leader offers a prayer, short, pointed, to the purpose; then reads a brief portion of Scripture. Ten minutes are now gone. Meantime requests in sealed envelopes have been going up to the desk for prayer. Every nook and corner is filled — the doorways and stairways — and the upper room is now filled, and we hear the voice of singing.

"A deep, solemn silence settles down upon our meeting. It is holy ground. The leader stands with slips of paper in his hand.

"He says 'This meeting is now open for prayer. Brethren from a distance are specially invited to take part, all will observe the rules.'

"All is now breathless attention. A tender solicitude spreads over all those upturned faces.

"The chairman reads, 'A son in North Carolina desires the fervent, effectual prayers of the righteous of this congregation for the immediate conversion of his mother in Connecticut.'

"In an instant a father rises, 'I wish to ask the prayers of this meeting for two sons and a daughter.

"And he sits down and bursts into tears, and lays his head down on the railing of the seat before him, and sobs like a broken-hearted child. We say in our heart, 'Oh heart-stricken parent! do you not know that these children are close by the kingdom.'

"A brother rises and pours out all his heart in prayer for that 'mother,' for those 'two sons' and 'that daughter.'

"A few remarks follow—very brief. The chairman rises with slips of paper in his hand, and reads, 'A praying sister requests prayers for two unconverted brothers in the city of Detroit; that they be converted and become true followers of the Lord Jesus Christ.'

"Another, 'Prayers are requested of the people of God for a young man, once a professor of religion, but now a wanderer, and going astray. These Christian parents invoke a continued interest in your prayers.'

"And another, from West Cornwall, Vt. 'Believing in the power and efficacy of prayer, an aged widowed mother requests the prayers of those Christians who assemble for daily prayer, for the immediate conversion of two sons, that they may become the meek and humble followers of the meek and lowly Jesus. A sick daughter sincerely unites with her in this earnest request.'

"Two prayers in succession followed these requests — very fervent, very earnest. And others who rose to pray at the same time, sat down again when they found themselves preceded by the voices already engaged in prayer. Then arose from all hearts that beautiful hymn, sung with touching pathos, so appropriate, too, just in this stage of this meeting, with all these cases full before us —

> "'There is a fountain filled with blood
> Drawn from Immanuel's veins,
> And sinners plunged beneath that flood
> Lose all their guilty stains.'

"Then followed prayer by one who prays earnestly for all who have been prayed for, for all sinners present, for the perishing thousands in this city, for the spread of revivals all over the land and world.

"It is now a quarter to one o'clock. Time has fled on silver wings. The chairman rises again with still more slips in his hands, and reads, 'A resident of Georgia requests the prayers of this meeting for two dear brothers, that they may be brought to Christ in this day of salvation; one residing near this meeting, and the other three thousand miles away from the home of his childhood. Also for a dear and only child.'

"O! that mother, that mother — and all these mothers — shall they not see all these children converted?

"Again he reads, and this, like others, was very

affecting, 'May I, without presumption, prefer a request for myself, though only a private individual, and for a feeble church among whom my lot is cast, that we may be melted and humbled, and endued with power from on high, and made instrumental of salvation — establish His kingdom with power, and exalt His throne in the midst of us? Gird thy sword upon thy thigh, Oh, Thou Most Mighty!'

"'I would beg leave to prefer the same request for all the churches, some thirty in number, connected with this presbytery, being among the few reported at the late General Assembly wholly unvisited with the showers of grace. The request will not be considered out of season. My soul breaketh for the longing that it hath, so says one of our oldest ministers.'

"This was understood to be a presbytery in Virginia. Many eyes filled with tears when this request was read. And who will soon forget the prayer that followed for those unvisited churches and that humble petitioner.

"Then there arose a sailor, now one no more, by reason of ill-health, but daily laboring for sailors. He was converted on board a man-of-war, and he knew how hard it was for the converted sailor to stand up firm against the storm of jeers and reproaches, and taunts of a ship's crew. 'Now I am here,' he said, 'to represent one who has requested me to ask your prayers for a converted sailor, this day gone to sea. I parted from him a little time ago, and his fear is that he may dishonor the cause of the blessed Redeemer. Will you pray for this sailor?'

"Prayer was offered for his keeping and guidance.

"Then came the closing hymn, the benediction, and the parting for twenty-four hours."

CHAPTER XXXIII.

THE CHICAGO NOONDAY PRAYER-MEETING.*

THE year 1857 was as conspicuous throughout the country for its religious revival as for its commercial disasters. The revival swept over the country vitalizing dead churches, resulting in the conversion of thousands of people, and the organization of new churches and new religious associations in every quarter. The Young Men's Christian Association of New York was instituted Sept. 23, 1857. Elsewhere such associations were springing up and prospering, and these facts were not lost on the Christian men of this city. There already existed a Young Men's Society for Religious Improvement, and this society issued a call for a meeting of Christian men to be held in Me-

---

* I am indebted to Mr. W. W. Vamarsdale, editor of *The Watchman*, for the following interesting sketch. *The Watchman* is "the only international medium of communication" between the various "Young Men's Christian Associations of the United States and British Provinces," and is published by Mr. F. H. Revell, Chicago. This noonday meeting has a great interest because it was the school in which Mr. Moody labored for so many years, and in which he himself was so efficiently trained.

tropolitan Block for the purpose of establishing a noon prayer-meeting. This meeting was held in the latter part of November, and was largely attended. The noon meeting was at once established and drew large audiences for some time.

Among those persons who most actively participated in this initial movement were the Rev. R. W. Patterson, Rev. E. F. Dickinson, D.D., then and now city missionary; Rev. W. G. Howard, D.D., of the Baptist Church; Rev. Mr. Curtis, of the First Presbyterian Church; Rev. Noah Hunt Schenck, D.D., then of the Trinity Episcopal Church, now of Brooklyn; Rev. James Baum, Methodist Church, afterward sent to India; Rev. N. L. Rice, D.D., North Presbyterian; Messrs. J. V. Farwell, E. S. Wells, Tuthill King, T. B. Carter, H. G. Penfield, L. D. Boone, Samuel Hood, Cyrus Bentley, B. W. Rayman, W. H. Brown, C. N. Holden, W. C. Grant, B. F. Jacobs, P. L. Underwood. Sylvester Lind, and Alex. Fyfe.

The meetings were held in Metropolitan Hall, and were for weeks so thronged that hundreds of people were unable to gain admittance. In connection with these meetings a series of sermons were preached by the Rev. R. W. Patterson, D.D., the Rev. James E. Foy, the Rev. Noah Hunt Schenck, D.D., the Rev. Mr. Rice, and others.

Toward the latter part of the winter the attendance fell off greatly, in great part because other prayer-meetings were being held all over the city. In the spring the attendance often fell to a dozen or two, and sometimes to two or three, but Alexander Fyfe was always on hand, and the meetings were not suspended, but as they no longer required a large hall they were moved to the basement of the First Baptist Church, which stood where the Chamber of Commerce now is.

The B. Y. M. C. A. was organized May 17, 1858, with Cyrus Bentley as President. Then, the noon prayer-meeting being in a very low state, and its dissolution being in prospect, unless some change was made, it was adopted by the association late in the spring of 1858, and moved from the First Baptist Church to Lind's Block on Randolph street, where the association had its rooms.

During the war the prayer-meeting was again largely attended, and wielded a powerful influence. It was the centre from which emanated wide-spread efforts not only to supply the spiritual wants of the soldiers, but also to alleviate their physical sufferings.

It was in the noon prayer-meeting that Messrs. D. L. Moody and B. F. Jacobs broached the subject of a building for the Christian Association. The effort to obtain a second building was originated in the same place. A couple of years after the fire a statement in a city paper that the association gave no signs of life and appeared to have outlived its usefulness, read in the noon prayer-meeting by Mr Jacobs, aroused the friends of the association to the necessities of the hour, and the meeting decided to raise $5,000 and put up a temporary building on the old lot. The $5,000 came so easily that the efforts to raise the money were continued, and the present building is the result.

In 1868 Mr. Jacobs was working for the adoption of uniform Sunday-school lessons, an idea then very generally opposed. As a move in this direction, the Saturday noon meeting was made a teachers' meeting, for the study of the next day's lesson. This was the first meeting of the kind in the country. There are now twenty-six of them.

· Mr. Moody began to take an active interest in the noon meeting and the association in 1859. For some time a good part of the attendance at the noon meeting was due to his personal effort.

The writer of this article first attended the meetings in 1868, and well remembers Mr. Moody's personal appeal to attend regularly, and confess Christ before men. Although an entire stranger to him, the words were heeded and resulted in a greater blessing to the writer than any other meetings he has ever attended. During the last twenty-one years of this meeting, not a day has been missed, even after the great fire of 1871. Mr. Moody held the meeting on the West Side, in the American Reformed Church, while the fire was still raging.

In 1873-4 Maj. J. N. Cole labored very earnestly in behalf of the meeting in advertising it in the hotels, cars and on the streets, which resulted in a largely increased attendance and excellent meetings. During 1876-7, the attendance averaged over two hundred, daily, making it the best attended meeting in this country. The attendance at present is a little over one hundred, daily.

In these meetings on Fridays, the subject is temperance, and on Saturdays, the Sunday-school lesson for the following day.

As it is a matter of general profit to know how a large and successful prayer-meeting is conducted, the invitation sent to the leader, and the directions to guide him, are herewith annexed, and need no other words of comment or explanation :

YOUNG MEN'S CHRISTIAN ASSOCIATION.

CHICAGO, 150 Madison St., —— 187 .

Dear Brother —

Will you lead the Noonday Prayer-Meeting, on .... the .... from 12 to 12:45 o'clock P. M.

Please reply by return of mail, noting your topic or subject for the meeting, and oblige.

Yours very truly,

.... Secretary.

To ....

N. B. — Topic suggested for this day by the International Committee of the Y. M. C. A. is

If another subject should seem more appropriate you are at liberty to use it.

It is desirable that the leader should be at the rooms a few minutes before the time for commencing the meeting.

ORDER OF EXERCISES.

Be prompt.

The opening exercises of the meeting must not exceed twenty minutes, including Singing, Prayer, Reading Scriptures and Remarks of Leader.

1. Open the meeting by giving out a hymn, or part of one.
2. Prayer by the leader, or some one in the audience, on whom he may call for that purpose.
3. Reading of Scripture and remarks of leader.
4. Announce: The meeting is now open for prayers and ex-

hortations — observing particularly the three minute rule. Invite the strangers present to take part in the services.

5. Request the brethren leading in prayer to remember especially all the careless and impenitent, also the anxious and inquiring, who may be present at this meeting.

6. Call for all the requests at the opening of the meeting — requiring a prayer to follow next after reading the same, having special reference to such requests.

7 All written requests left on the desks or otherwise, should be handed to a member of the devotional committee, and presented to the meeting by him.

8. At intervals when there is a hesitancy in the meeting, give out one verse of a hymn.

9. In case of any debatable suggestion or proposition by any person, say: This is simply a prayer-meeting, and that would be out of order. Call on some brother to pray.

10. Give out the closing hymn in time to let the people depart by 12:45 o'clock, sharp.

RULES.

Prayers or remarks should not exceed three minutes.

Not more than two prayers or two addresses should follow each other.

Request all who take part in the meeting to face the audience and speak in a clear distinct tone.

CHAPTER XXXIV.

Prayer-Meeting Conventions.

PRESIDENT Edwards has devoted a treatise, (Vol. 3. 429) to "A humble attempt to promote explicit agreement and visible union of God's people in extraordinary prayer, for the revival of religion and the advancement of Christ's kingdom on earth, pursuant to Scripture promises and prophesies concerning the *last time.*" In part first he opens the text, "Thus saith the Lord of Hosts. It shall come to pass, that there shall come people, and the inhabitants of many cities, and the inhabitants of one city shall go to another, saying, Let us go speedily to pray before the Lord, and to seek the Lord of Hosts: I will go also. Yea, many people and strong nations shall come to seek the Lord of Hosts in Jerusalem, and to pray before the Lord."—Zech. 8: 20-22. To this is subjoined a memorial on "Union in Prayer," issued Aug. 26, 1746, by several ministers in Scotland, to their brethren in different places, for continuing a concert for prayer, first entered into in 1744. In part second, motives to a compliance with what is proposed in the memorial are presented. In part third, some objections are answered. The whole piece concludes with a pointed summary, in way of application, to the principles that have been discussed.

We may suppose there are suggestions here which point toward the holding of prayer-meeting conventions. At any rate we find that attempts have been made to carry out the spirit of the text which is made the key-note to this treatise by President Edwards. It is stated by Rev. J. B. Johnston that the Reformed churches (United Presbyterian, etc.,) during the period of Union, held eight conventions of this nature between 1838 and 1846, for the purpose of uniting in prayer, and others religious exercises. His account of the prayer-meeting convention that met in Xenia, Ohio, 1858, is particularly full and instructive. In the circular, issued as a call for that convention, among other things a few topics were suggested as appropriate subjects of consideration on an occasion of this kind:

1. The true nature of a revival.
2. Indications of the need of a revival.
3. Encouragements to hope for a revival.
4. Causes of the present deadness of the church.
5. Sins of the day as impeding the progress of religion.
6. Means of promoting revival.
7. Necessity for the influences of the Holy Spirit.

8. Evidences of a true revival.

9. Revival of religion essential to the success of missions.

10. Aspects of Divine Providence toward the Church and the world.

This convention met as it had been invited to do, and spent a few days in most Christian fellowship and profitable discussion. The results were summed up as follows by a special committee, to be:

"*Resolved*, That it is the duty of the convention to give an expression to our churches in regard to the specific measures which should be adopted by our sessions and members, so that a proper direction may be given to the present awakening on the subject of religion. While we have no new measures to recommend, it may be proper for us to set about the use of God's measures and means with new life and vigor; these are the faithful, direct preaching of the Word, earnest prayer to God in the closet, in the family and in the social meeting — opening our churches for prayer through the week, where the circumstances of our people, and the need of the community, render such a measure expedient. Establishing meetings for prayer and conference in as many localities as possible — urging on our members and elders the duty of taking an active part in these meetings."

A convention was also held, after this, in the city of Allegheny, but the expectations of most who met were disappointed. Said one of the speakers, "I confess that the conference has not come up to my own feelings as to what it should be. What is the reason? What is it that arrests, so often, the growing interest? What is it that dampens so often the rising fervor of devotion? It is the inordinate concern about an event anticipated in the future."

Now, may I not give a practical conclusion to this chapter? What shall prevent God's people, those who love to pray, and who relish the blessings of spiritual communion, from assembling in a prayer-meeting conference, just as those deeply interested in Sabbath-schools meet from time to time in institutes and county or State conventions? Would it not be highly edifying and stimulating, whilst avoiding all appearance of fanaticism, to meet for the study of the Bible on, say particularly, such subjects as are outlined in the above circular? "Let us go speedily to pray before the Lord and to seek the Lord of Hosts: I will go also."

Or, failing to find continued necessity for such conferences, on the part of all the people, Methodists have their district conferences, Baptists their associations, Congregationalists their conventions, Lutherans their synods, Presbyterians their presbyteries, and so on; why may not a part of their various exercises be to consider these very things? What things? Why such subjects as these, "The Bible History of Prayer," "The Prayers of the Bible," "Bible Answers to Prayer," "Prayer and its Remarkable Answers in Our Day," "The Power of Prayer," "The Philosophy of Prayer," "The True Prayer-Gauge," "Gospel Means and Methods for Revivals," "Narratives of Remarkable Conversions and Revival Incidents," "Five Years of Prayer," "Fifteen Years of Prayer," "The Church Prayer-Meeting And Its Improvement," and "How To Conduct Prayer-Meetings."

Do you not think that the direct and associated study of such subjects, year by year, the appearing before the Lord in concerted prayer, and the seeking of the Holy Spirit for growth in grace and reviving, would be eminently feasible, practical and full of spiritual blessings to the church collectively, and to her membership individually?

CHAPTER XXXV.

"DIRECTORY FOR WORSHIP OF THE UNITED PRESBYTERIAN CHURCH.

"PRAYER-Meetings: 1. Meetings for prayer should be held in every congregation. Matt. 3: 16, etc. —Acts 2:4 etc. When a minister is present, he should preside, and give direction to the exercises. In his absence, an elder, or member of approved piety, should conduct the meeting.

"2. The exercises should consist of reading the Scriptures, the singing of Psalms, the offering of suitable prayers, and remarks founded on some passage of Scripture, or interesting event of Providence. The whole should conduct to brotherly love, personal piety, and the general interests of religon.

"3. Meetings for prayer may be held at one or more times, and in one or more places, in the congregation during the week. But they should never be allowed to interfere with, or to take the place of, important religious duties in the family.

"4. Church sessons should hold a sessional prayer-meeting at least once a month, at which they may consult about the condition and interests of the flock, and implore divine guidance in all that to which they are called.

"5. When a congregation has no pastor, or when he is absent, it may be profitable to spend a part of the Sabbath in social prayer; and if none are present capable of making appropriate remarks, let some one read an evangelical and instructive sermon.

" Church officers should exhort the people to a faithful attendance on prayer-meetings, and none should excuse themselves from attending, without good reason."

CHAPTER XXXVI.

Moody's Seventeen Rules for Keeping up the Interest.

THERE are some in every church, most likely, who will come to the prayer-meeting, if there is an unusual interest in its exercises. If they hear that something new is characterizing the meetings, they have a curiosity to go and see for themselves. As soon as the interest abates, they again drop out. It is my experience, as that of others, that the prayer-meeting requires constant labor for its improvement. It may be brought to a high state of excellence, and a few weeks of letting things run themselves will destroy it all, and leave matters just where they were before.

"Since beginning my work here," writes the Rev. Herbert W. Lathe, pastor Plymouth Church, Portland, Me., "my prayer-meetings have been my greatest anxiety, and I have gone to work hard to improve them. I find that they will not 'go' of themselves. They need a great deal of careful thought and preparation. And the preparation which really prepares, in my experience, is, not merely the collection and arrangement of 'something to say,' but constant attention to all the details of the meeting, such as singing, variety of topic and method, etc. I sometimes speak to individuals, previous to the meetings, as to taking a part. I have found it helpful, occasionally, to distribute passages of Scripture, to individuals previously, and request them to repeat them at the meeting. At times I have requested all to bring their testaments, and have then given out passages to various persons (if possible such as do not usually take part), asking them to read. Once or twice I have presented the topic in the form of a question, or problem, and requested the brethren to give *their* views first. This I do when the subject is very simple and I fear that they would have nothing to say after me. For example, I presented Paul and James on 'Faith and Works,' and asked the brethren to reconcile them. Indeed, I am constantly devising expedients, careful not to forget that it is 'not by might, nor by power, but by my Spirit.' I am delighted that so much thought is being given to the prayer-meeting. It is the thermometer of the church."

Mr. Moody's directions for sustaining a continued interest in the social meetings for prayer, are in the line of these suggestions, and come from one who by a long experience has learned both how to do it, and how not to do it:

" 1. Get the people near together.

" 2. Let the meeting places be well ventilated.

" 3. Have some good singing.

" 4. When we have special meetings let us have special prayer.

" 5. Let requests be received for special cases.

" 6. Let the minister or leader presiding do little more than give the key-note to the service.

" 7. It is well to give out the next subject at the previous meeting.

" 8. Do not scold the people who have come because the rest have not come.

" 9. If we are discouraged, do not let any one see it.

" 10. Do not have more than two prayers consecutively.

" 11. Do not have a formal address.

" 12. Have the meeting short.

" 13. Avoid discussion.

" 14. If you can not get members to take part, go and speak to them about it alone.

" 15. Be sure and throw the meeting open half the time.

" 16. Be punctual.

" 17. Lastly, seek to make sure that in going to the meeting you are going to it in the Spirit.

CHAPTER XXXVII.

Different Forms of Printed Lists.

IT has seemed to me that it would prove quite a serviceable hint if I were to close this book with two or three specimen cards to show how the topics are most conveniently printed and prepared for circulation, among all the members of the congregation. It has been my custom to print the cards differently each year, so that the lists for the successive years might be easily distinguished from each other, and have the charm of novelty.

For example, for one year I printed on the first page the name of the church and its officers with a few words of explanation and of invitation; and on the fourth page some "Hints for the Improvement of our Prayer-Meeting." For another year a change was made in the size of the cards, in the kind of types used, and in the explanations on the first and fourth pages. A change of this kind does not add to the expense of printing, and makes the cards fresh and attractive for each year. It is well to print the subjects rather than merely announce them from the pulpit, so that in addition to other advantages, all who are unable to attend the meeting, whether from infirmity of age, or sickness, or for other reason, may know what themes are presented from week to week, and on the evening for prayer, though absent in body, they may truly be present in spirit. These lists, likewise, if preserved, will contain a history of the prayer-meeting in the church from year to year, in connection with which, those who have attended, will be enabled to recall in outline the remarks offered at those several meetings.

The following schedules, printed as nearly like the original, as the types will permit, present in a forcible manner these differences in type, size and looks. As they fully explain themselves, no comments are necessary.

Prayer-Meeting.

Thursday Evening 7:30 o'clock.

———

Themes for 1879.

SECOND

Presbyterian

CHURCH.

———

Wm. Alvin Bartlett.

PASTOR.

DIFFERENT FORMS OF PRINTED LISTS. 317

Jan.   2. The Talents,   Matt. 25: 14-30.
      9. Prayer for Nations Rulers and People,
         1 Tim. 2: 1-4.
     16. Backsliding Children,   Jer. 3: 14-15.
     23. A Clean Heart,   Ps. 15: 10-11.
     30. Prayer for the Young,   1 Chron.
        29. 18-28.
Feb.   6 God is Love,   1 John 4: 8.
     13. The World for Christ,   Acts 1: 1-8.
     20. The Ministry of Reconciliation, 2 Cor.
        5; 18.
     27. Remembrance of Mercies, Ps. 71: 14-24.
Mar.   6. A Man Sought,   Jer. 5: 1.
     13. "Are there few that be saved?" Luke
        13: 23-28.
     20. Blessed are the Pure in Heart," Matt.
        5: 8.
     27. Beautiful Zion,   Ps. 50: 2.
April   3. Woman's Work,   Rom. 16: 1-13.
     10. Prayer for the Gospel,   2 Thes. 3:1.
     17. Godly Sorrow,   2 Cor. 7:10.
     24. Broken Cisterns,   Jer. 2: 13.
May   1. Highways and Hedges, Matt. 22: 1-10.
     8. The Widow of Nain,   Luke 7: 11-16.
     15. The Cleansing Blood,   1 John 1:7.
     22. Living Honestly,   Rom. 3: 7-14.
     29. Search the Scriptures,   John 5:39.
June   5. Certainty of Salvation, 1 Peter 1: 1-9.
     12. Rest,   Heb. 4: 1-9.
     19. The Transfiguration,   Matt. 17: 1-8.
     26. The Greatest,   Luke 22: 24-27.

July	3. Does Sin Pay?	Rom. 6:21.
	10. Family Prayer,	1 Cor. 16:19.
	17. "Am I my Brother's keeper?"	Gen. 4:9.
	24. The Sons of God in the World,	Phil. 2:15.
	31. The Prodigal,	Luke 15:11-32.
Aug.	7. Ruth,	Book of Ruth.
	14. Old Paths Rejected,	Jer. 6:16.
	21. Jesus and the Resurrection,	Acts 17:18.
	28. The Barren Fig Tree,	Luke 13:6-9.
Sept.	4. Will a Man Rob God,	Matt. 3:7-10.
	11. The Lamb of God,	John 1:29.
	18. Christian Courtesy, Ruth 2:4,	Gal. 6:1-2.
	25. At Jesus' Feet,	Luke 10:39.
Oct.	2. "Come ye Blessed,"	Matt. 25:34-46.
	9. Promises,	2 Peter 1:4.
	16. "Satan Came also,"	Job 1:6.
	23. The Comforter,	John 14:16-26.
	30. The Lord can save by many or by few, 1 Sam. 14:6.	
Nov.	6. The Minimum of faith,	Num. 21:5-9.
	13. Jesus before Pilate,	Matt. 27.
	20. Give Thanks,	Ps. 147:1-20.
	27. Faith,	Heb. 11.
Dec.	4. Naaman,	2 Kings 5.
	11. The poor,	John 12:5.
	18. Death and Victory,	1 Cor. 15:55-56.
	25. Bethlehem,	Luke 2.

SERVICES.
    Sabbath Morning and Evening.

SACRAMENT SABBATHS ⎧ Last Sun. in Jan.
                    ⎪   "   "   Mar.
Baptism & Lord's Supper ⎨   "   "   June.
                    ⎩   "   "   Oct.
    Preparatory Service the Preceding Friday.

SABBATH SCHOOL.
    At 2:15 P. M. Teachers' Meeting Thursday
        Evening 7:00, before Prayer-Meeting.

PRAYER-MEETING.
    Sabbath Morning, 9:30.
    Thursday Evening, 7:30.
    Young Peoples' Monday Evening, 7:30.

SESSION MEETING.
    First Tuesday Evening of each month, and after each Tuesday Evening Prayer-Meeting.

DEACON'S MEETING.
    Alternate Monday Evenings.

COLLECTIONS.
    Third Sabbath Morning of each month.
    For the Poor on Sacrament Sabbaths.

ANNUAL MEETING OF CHURCH & CONGREGATION.
    First Thursday Evening in January after Prayer-Meeting.

BRICK CHURCH,

ROCHESTER, N. Y.

Rev. JAMES B. SHAW, D.D., Pastor.

Elder DAVID DICKEY,
" LOUIS CHAPIN,
" HARVEY C. FENN,
" EDWIN SCRANTOM,
" CHARLES F. WEAVER,
" LANSING G. WETMORE,
" JESSE W. HATCH,
" GEORGE N. STORMS,
" JOEL G. DAVIS,
" EDWARD WEBSTER,
} Session.

THE design of this Schedule, in which this Church unites with many others, is to make more of our CHURCH PRAYER-MEETING; to secure a larger attendance, and a more general participation in the exercises, and thus to add to its interest and spiritual power. Should a particular Providence at any time call our thoughts to other subjects, this order will be suspended.

It has been adopted as an aid to united, intelligent Conference and Prayer; not to prevent a devout consideration of any subject that is just then of special interest, or to compel any one to speak upon the topic or be silent. It is intended not to bring into bondage, but to give liberty, by leading to a study of the Word, and a preparation for the Meeting.

☞ Keep this Schedule in the Bible you daily use.

DIFFERENT FORMS OF PRINTED LISTS. 321

TOPICS FOR 1879.

Jan. 1. A Seasonable Exhortation. Isa. 62 : 6, 7.
" 5-12. WEEK OF PRAYER. Baptism of the Holy Ghost.
" 15. All Things Ready. Matt. 22 : 1-4.
" 22. The Servant's Commission. Matt. 22 : 9.
" 29. Prayer for Schools. Isa. 54. 13; Prov. 22 : 6; Hosea 4 : 6.
Feb. 5. Monthly Concert. China and the Chinese in America.
" 12. Christ's Laborers. Matt. 20 : 1-16; Acts 9 : 6; I. Cor. 3 : 9.
" 19. Without God no Success. Ps. 127 : 1; John 15 : 5; 6 : 63.
" 26. With Him no Failure. Phil. 4 ; 13; II. Cor. 3 : 5.
Mar. 5. Monthly Concert. Mexico and New Mexico.
" 12. Christ our Passover. Exodus 12; I. Cor. 5 : 7 ; John 1 : 29.
" 19. Public Confession Required. Romans. 10 : 10; Matt. 10 : 32, 33 ; Acts 16 : 33.
" 26. Profession without Hypocrisy. Acts 19 : 18, 19; II. Cor. 5 : 14, 15.
Apr. 2. Monthly Concert. India.
" 9. Rising with Christ. Luke 24 : 34; Col. 3 : 1; I. Cor. 15 : 14.
" 16. Seed Sowing. Gal. 6 : 7, 8; Eccl. 11 : 6; Psalm 126 : 6.
" 23. Answered while Praying. Dan. 9; 21-3; Acts 12 : 5-10; Luke 23 : 42, 43.
" 30. Temperance. Eph. 5 : 18: Rom. 14 : 21 ; Psalm 94 : 20.
May 7. Monthly Concert. Siam and Laos.
" 14. God our Refuge. Ps. 46.
" 21. The House Swept and Garnished. Luke 11 : 25.
" 28. Witness of the Spirit. Rom. 8 : 16.
Jun 4. Monthly Concert. Africa.
" 11. Children's Claim on the Church. Ps. 78 : 5.
" 18. Our Enjoyment Pleasing to God. I. Tim 6 : 17.
" 25. Self Denial. Matt. 16 : 24, 25.

TOPICS FOR 1879.

July 2. Monthly Concert. North American Indians.
" 9. Declaration of Dependence. Josh, 24 : 21–27.
" 16. The Great Harvest. Matt. 13 : 39; John 4 : 35, 36.
" 23. Be Faithful. Luke 16 : 10–12; Rev. 2 : 10.
" 30. Rest after work. Mark 6 : 31 ; Ps. 127 : 2.
Aug. 6. Monthly Concert. South America.
" 13. Christ with the Twos and Threes. Matt. 18 : 20.
" 20. The Rock Shadow. Isa. 32 : 2.
" 27. Watchfulness. Matt. 24 : 42. 26 : 40.
Sep. 3. Monthly Concert. Japan.
" 10. The Faithful Christian. John 15 : 8.
" 17. What brought me to Christ? John 1 : 42. 6 : 44. I. Cor. 12 : 6.
" 24. Am I Growing in Grace? II. Peter 3 : 18.
Oct. 1. Monthly Concert. Persia.
" 8. Nothing can Save but Christ. John 14 : 6; Acts 4 : 12.
" 15. He Saves all who Come unto Him. John 6 : 37 ; Rev. 22 : 17.
" 22. All such Become Like Him. Rom. 8, 9 ; Matt. 10 : 38; I. John 3 : 3.
" 29. The Christian Citizen. Acts 22, 27, 28 ; I. Cor. 10 : 31.
Nov. 5. Monthly Concert. Papal Europe.
" 12. The Sure Choice. Josh 24 : 15 ; II. Peter 1 : 10.
" 19. Speaking for Christ. Mal. 3 : 16 ; Heb. 10 : 25.
" 26. All things ours. I. Cor. 3 : 21, 22.
Dec. 3. Monthly Concert. Syria.
" 10. Piety in Home Life. I. Tim. 5 : 1–4 ; Eph. 6 ; 1–6.
" 17. Opportunities Neglected. Acts 24 : 24–27 ; 26 : 28.
" 24. The Advent. Isa. 9 : 6 ; Luke 2 : 7–14.
" 31. The End. I. Peter 4 : 7 ; II. Tim. 4 : 6, 7 ; I. Cor. 15 : 24.

PRACTICAL SUGGESTIONS.

Consider Wednesday evening engaged to attend the meeting, and plan accordingly. Suffer nothing to keep you away that would not be sufficient to keep you from a business engagement, or a social party. Persuade others to attend. If you have company, invite them to come with you. Bring the children. Come from your closet, if you have but a few minutes to spend there. Sit as far in front as possible. Give attention during the week to the topic. Look out corresponding passages of Scripture and study them. Try to be prepared to say something to the point, even if it be no more than to repeat an appropriate text. Be short whether you speak or pray. Allow no long pauses, to kill the life of the meeting. If your mind is strongly drawn to some other subject, yield to the influence, and speak as the Spirit may give utterance.

Feel that you are in your Father's house, with your brothers and sisters, brought together by His invitation to promote each other's spiritual welfare and enjoyment. Do not fear criticism, or ever indulge in it. Remember that not one in a thousand finds it easy to speak or to pray at first, and that in proportion to the effort necessary to overcome embarrassment has been the success and eminence obtained by many Christian workers. Consent to be habitually silent only after making the most strenuous and repeated endeavors to acquire self-possession. You may be a very useful Christian and yet be unheard here, but if you *can* overcome your infirmity, it will greatly increase your usefulness.

Do your part to make the meeting aid in the cultivation of a social, friendly spirit. Address strangers in words of welcome and kindness. Linger at the close to take each other by the hand, and to manifest an interest in the personal welfare of your fellow worshippers. This cannot be done, to any extent, upon the Sabbath, because of the immediate opening of the Sabbath-school and for other reasons; but this meeting affords an opportunity for sociability that should by no means be neglected. But be careful that the sociability does not degenerate into mere secular chat. Let it deepen, not diminish or destroy, the spiritual feeling that has been quickened.

"*Now, unto Him that is able to do exceeding abundantly above all that we ask or think according to the power that worketh in us, unto Him be glory in the Church by Christ Jesus throughout all ages, world without end. Amen.*"

SUBJECTS

FOR THE

WEEKLY PRAYER-MEETINGS,

OF THE

SECOND PRESBYTERIAN CHURCH,

PEORIA, ILLINOIS.

Held in the Lecture Room every Wednesday Evening.

1880.

REV. LEWIS O. THOMPSON, Pastor.

ELDERS:

JOHN C. GRIER.	DAVID McCULLOCH.
JOHN A. McCOY.	ARTHUR A. RUGG.

God has said: "My house shall be called an House of Prayer." He has commanded: "Forsake not the assembling of yourselves together, as the manner of some is." It is recorded: "They that feared the Lord spake often one to another." It is a matter of experience: "While they communed together, Jesus himself drew near." In view of divine commands, promises, and blessings such as these, I hereby pledge myself to be a regular attendant at our Prayer-Meeting, and to bring as many with me as I can. I am not weary in well-doing.

(Signed.)

Subjects for the Prayer-Meeting.

1880.

JANUARY.

7—Good Paths for the New Year.   Jer. vi: 16.   Prov. 3: 17.
14—Foreign Missions. General Review.   Ex xlvii:4-5.
21—Absence from the Prayer-Meeting attended with loss.   John xx: 24.
28—Preface to the Ten Commandments.   Ex. xx: 2.

FEBRUARY.

4—Monthly Concert. China and the Chinese in California. Luke ii: 32.
11—Beatitude for the poor in spirit.   Matt. v: 3.
18—A first duty of the converted.   Luke xxii: 32.
25—The First Commandment.   Ex. xx: 3.   Is. xliii: 10-15.

MARCH.

3—Monthly Concert. Mexico.   Mal. i: 11.
10—Beatitude for those that mourn.   Matt. v: 4.
17—The continuance of the Spirit with the Church.   John xiv: 16-17. II. Cor. xiii: 14.
24—Promises fulfilled in Christ.   II. Cor. i: 20.
31—The Second Commandment.   Ex. xx: 4-6. Col. iii: 1-5.

APRIL.

7—Monthly Concert. India.   Rom. vi: 23.
14—Beatitude for the meek.   Matt. v: 5.
21—The choice of Moses.   Heb. xi: 24-27
28—The Third Commandment.   Ex. xx: 7. Matt. v: 33-37.

MAY.

5—Monthly Concert. Siam and Laos.   Is. ii: 8.
12—Beatitude for those that hunger and thirst.   Matt. v: 6.
19—A Promise Meeting.   II. Chron. vii: 14-15
26—The Fourth Commandment.   Ex. xx. 8-11. Jer. xvii: 19-27.

JUNE.

2—Monthly Concert. Africa.   Num. xiv: 21.
9—Special Providence.   Ps. xxxvii: 23.
16—The Home Field.   Luke xxiv: 47.
23—Mizpah.   Gen. xxxi: 49.
30—The Fifth Commandment.   Ex. xx: 12. Luke ii. 51.

JULY.

7—Monthly Concert. NORTH AMERICAN INDIANS. Num. xiii: 30. Deut. i: 21.
14—Beatitude for the merciful. Matt. v: 7.
21—Consecration Meeting. Ex. xxxii: 29. Rom. xii: 1-2. Col. iii: 2.
28—The Sixth Commandment. Ex. xx: 13. Matt. v: 21-22.

AUGUST.

4—Monthly Concert. SOUTH AMERICA. Is. lii: 10.
11—Beatitude for the pure in heart. Matt. v: 8.
18—The Christians' life-force. John xiv: 19.
25—The Seventh Commandment. Ex. xx: 14. Eph. v: 3-7.

SEPTEMBER.

1—Monthly Concert. JAPAN. Micah iv: 2.
8—Beautitude for peacemakers. Matr. v: 9.
15—Self-denial. Matt. xvi: 24. Gal. v: 24.
22—Connection between faith and the sanctification of the Spirit. II. Thess. ii: 13.
29—The Eighth Commandment. Ex. xx: 15. Lev. xix: 11-13.

OCTOBER.

6—Monthly Concert. PERSIA. Ps. xxxvi: 9.
13—Beatitude for those that are persecuted. Matt. v: 10-12.
20—"Is life worth living?" Matt. xvi: 26. Matt. xxvi: 24.
27—The Ninth Commandment. Ex. xx: 16. Ps. xv: 1-4.

NOVEMBER.

3—Monthly Concert. PAPAL EUROPE. Rev. ii: 4-5.
10—Man as helper in divine work. John xi: 39, 44.
17—The Tenth Commandment. Ex. xx: 17. Heb. xiii: 5.
24—Thanksgiving Meeting. I. Chron. xxix: 10-19.

DECEMBER.

1—Monthly Concert. SYRIA. Acts xiii: 16-41.
8—Exaggeration and swearing forbidden. Matt. v: 33-37.
15—A Promise Meeting. Jer. xxix: 13. Matt. vi: 24.
22—Comprehensive summary of the Ten Commandments. Matt. xxii: 36-40.
29—"All's well that ends well." Job xlii: 10-17.

The Second Presbyterian Church

MADISON ST., COR. JACKSON.

Public Worship, Sunday Morning and Evening.
Sabbath School, Sunday Morning, 9:30.
Meeting of Session, first Monday of each month.
"Light Bearers," Mission Band of Sabbath School, meets second Sabbath of each month.
Prayer-Meeting, Wednesday Evening.
Ladies' Prayer-Meeting, Friday afternoon.
Ladies' Foreign Missionary Society, meets monthly, on Friday.
Teachers' Meeting meets weekly, on Saturday.
Church Socials, monthly through the year.
Industrial School Saturday Afternoon.
Choir-Meeting Saturday Evening.
Sunday Prayer-Meeting Sunday Evening before service.
Communion, second Sunday in January, April, June and October. Preparatory Service on Friday Evening preceding.
Children's Sunday, Sunday following the Communion.

SUNDAY SCHOOL.

ARTHUR H. RUGG, Supt. S. S. WINN, Ass't Supt.
GEO. BRYAN, Sec. & Treas. Col. J. D. McCLURE Librarian.

www.ingramcontent.com/pod-product-compliance
Lightning Source LLC
Chambersburg PA
CBHW030736230426
43667CB00007B/729